LEAST LOVED BEASTS OF THE REALLY WILD WEST

A TRIBUTE

EDITED BY

TERRIL L. SHORB

AND

YVETTE A. SCHNOEKER-SHORB

NATIVE WEST PRESS

LEAST LOVED BEASTS
OF THE *REALLY* WILD WEST:
A TRIBUTE

A Native West Press Book
July 1997

ISBN 0-9653849-0-X
Library of Congress Catalog
Card Number 96-69432
1. Nature in Literature 2. Animals in Literature 3. Nature Study—Poetry 4. Animals—Poetry

Cover/Title Page Photography: © 1997 Terril Shorb
Editors: Terril L. Shorb and Yvette A. Schnoeker-Shorb
Contributing Editor: Mary Anne McDaniel
Design: Amanda Summers
Production: Triad Associates
Printed by Courier Graphics Corporation

For information please contact:
Native West Press, P.O. Box 12227,
Prescott, AZ 86304.

Manufactured in the United States of America
Printed on recycled paper

ACKNOWLEDGMENTS

"The Creatures on My Mind" copyright © 1990 by Ursula K. Le Guin; from *Unlocking the Air and Other Stories* (HarperCollins); first appeared in *Harper's*; reprinted by permission of the author and the author's agent, Virginia Kidd.

"The Lesson" copyright © 1996 by Jim Nollman; first appeared in *The Interspecies Newsletter;* reprinted by permission of the author.

"Woven Symbiosis" copyright © 1996 by Matt Welter; first appeared in *Yellowstone 88* (Hodge Podge Press); reprinted by permission of the author.

"Magpie" copyright © 1996 by Bill Yake; from *Givin' Critters Short Shrift*; first appeared in *Blue Light Review*; reprinted by permission of the author and Radiolarian Press.

"Mountain Goat" copyright © 1996 by Bill Yake; from *Givin' Critters Short Shrift*; reprinted by permission of the author and Radiolarian Press.

TABLE OF CONTENTS

INTRODUCTION

Many of us carry around in the worn wallet of memory snapshots of wild animal faces. Fawns, bunnies, or red-breasted robins bring a smile to our own. Other faces, however, sometimes summon shudders of revulsion, even abject terror: rats, bats, spiders, slugs, and snakes are often among people's least favorite creatures.

Why? Morphology, perhaps, is implicated. For in the conduct of creature-to-creature relations, familiarity usually breeds contentment. Communing with someone who has more eyes or fewer legs can be simply unnerving at first. Parental, popular, and cultural conditioning may also be factors. How many of us have memories of Dad swooping down on a hapless spider, smashing it before our startled eyes, leading us to believe that all little eight-leggers must be truly dangerous? Hollywood, too, has shaped our perceptions of those critters who do not have forward-facing, big, brown eyes. Tarantulas have been cast as the villains in movies as often as guys in black hats. One would think from their movie roles that rattlesnakes spend their days coiled, tails wagging, just waiting for opportunities to menace humans wherever they walk. The absence of positive roles is another way that certain creatures have been denied equal status. How come there are no movies with raccoons or scrub jays or Gila monsters as heroes?

It is not because these creatures lack character or beauty, or that they don't create splendid lives for themselves as they raise families, bask in the sun, dream in cozy burrows in the womb of the Earth.

Likely, these creatures are less loved because they are less known to us. Our dark imaginings have kept us away from them. Negative qualities attributed to the least loved beasts who inhabit our mindscapes do not describe the true nature of the creatures out in the wildscape. So what might happen if we venture to know these creatures better?

The collection you hold in your hands holds some answers to that interesting possibility. What follows are tributes to an astonishing variety of creatures: coyotes to cockroaches, rattlesnakes to rats, bats to javelina, crane flies to vultures. The writers themselves present a splendid diversity of livelihoods: zoologist to elementary school teacher, psychiatrist to computer programmer, accountant to social worker, historian to dream researcher.

We are grateful to our writers for their courage to stand against the tide of social convention and to proclaim their affections for wild creatures who have been banished from the complicated habitat of the human heart. The effect of these tributes is to give us hope for a human reconciliation with the natural world. For in learning to love the diversity of life forms on our world, we rediscover it in its fullest expression of living beauty. And in this broader, deeper appreciation is the promise of paradise regained.

THE EDITORS

PART ONE

RELATIVE REFLECTIONS ON LEAST LOVED BEASTS IN ALL WALKS OF LIFE

MANIFEST DESTINY LINGERS

1

Sitting sipping morning coffee   brother and I
sliding glass door open   California beach beyond.
Brother's sudden exclamation   "Oh my god!"
Alarmed, I wonder, "What? A tidal wave?"
"A huge spider just crawled in!"
It scurries behind stereo cabinet
brother pokes back there with broom handle
to no avail.

I recall   twelve years earlier
backpacking with him—South Fork Kings River.
From beneath jumbled boulders
snake rattle startles my wife.
I pull her back   and think that's the end of it.
But my brother   bent upon extermination
picks up long straight pine limb   jabs below rocks
fifteen minutes of maneuvering round for position
till, exasperated, "Son of a bitch got away."

In the morning   snake body stretched out
full length in granitic sand.
Brother pleased and relieved
one less vermin in the world.

2

Manifest destiny lingers   human minds blind
to the spirits of those who slither and crawl
across the ecstatic skin of the earth.

The lord's will?
This continent once oozed god's presence
now stripped of its enchantment.

Nature mind   balanced design
divine presence in the world declines
with each extinguished life.

God dwells   not only in the heavens
but in cool dark burrows
in nooks under rocks
and, sometimes
in human hearts.

by PAUL YOUNG

THE LESSON

It's four o'clock on a cloudy June afternoon. The air is heavy, the show of flowers beckons me outside to pay homage. After walking around for twenty minutes, paying special attention to the indeterminate color of a mounding blue cranesbill, sniffing the gallica roses, counting all the basil plants that are thriving, I enter that mindless mood of quiet admiration that occurs so often at this time of year. Finally I take a seat in a fold-up chair in the herb garden to watch the graceful tarragon swaying in a minimal breeze.

It's been an especially hard week. A wet spring has brought on a particularly bad allergy season, causing my nose to take on a life of its own. And just yesterday I received an email informing me that a major film about my work with animals, working with an eighty-year-old shaman in Central Asia who communicates to camels, has suddenly been canceled by the director with no explanation. I don't know how to respond—how does anyone know how to respond to people who use non-communication as their primary means of communication? It's like trying to talk to the dead. Nonetheless, I've spent the afternoon trying to figure how to do it; after all, the film would have kept me busy all next summer. Evidently, the shaman was filmed using overtone chants to inform a camel of the death of its keeper. The camel cried real tears. On camera.

So many weighty thoughts. My latest book is finally finished after a year of rewrites. It's a departure, a stretch, a kind of anti-adventure story—exploring the more surrealistic aspects of humans living for weeks in wilderness—like treating boredom as a form of grace. But the book is risky for a publisher. It has been accepted in New York and praised by the editor, but now I worry about all the ways it will get manhandled by the marketing department.

An inch-long caterpillar suddenly appears on the garden bed in front of me. It must have fallen from the plum tree directly above my head where, clearly, it was up to no good munching on ripe shoots. It starts traipsing across the bed. I bend my head, observe it closely, watch its body fluids flow back and forth inside its translucent green skin, offering a perfect lesson in hydraulics. By tensing the muscles in its rear end, the fluids flow to the front, causing its head to thrust stiffly upward and fore. It drops its head, grabs the dirt with its front hooks, and pulls the rest of its body along. A brief moment of rest causes the fluids to flow back to its hind end in preparation for the next step. What a dance!

A red ant appears and, without any hesitation, attacks the much larger caterpillar, sinking its sharp incisors right into the caterpillar's face. Ah, nature! The caterpillar answers by writhing forcefully, and then making a concerted effort to pry the ant off by levering it against the dirt. But this ant is not to be pried; now that the ant's incisors have grabbed hold, there is little the caterpillar can do to extricate it. I stare harder. For some reason, it seems important to discover if this ant has simply started eating the living caterpillar or, if instead, it is attempting to cut off a piece of flesh to carry back to the anthill. A second ant appears, grabs hold of the caterpillar's mid-section. The caterpillar starts writhing in earnest. No matter that it makes no sound, I easily imagine it shrieking in horrible pain until the neighbors start calling.

A third ant appears. The new arrival causes a change in dynamic. Now, the caterpillar seems to sense its own impending doom in no uncertain terms. It knows precisely what to do. Each time the new ant attempts to grab hold of the larger insect's tail, the caterpillar whips back and forth with a power I have not yet seen displayed. The new ant is getting nowhere. Each time it gets whipped around and deposited several inches from the fray, it retaliates by walking directly away from the caterpillar. Then it turns part way, as if deliberating what to do next. Maybe this deliberation is hard-wired. No amount of punishment seems able to deter it from attacking again.

This drama of the caterpillar and the three ants continues, without abatement, and without any change in tactics, for another half hour. At one point, a new species of ant appears, this one shiny and purple-black, displaying much faster, less deliberate movements. It rushes toward the caterpillar, but then suddenly seems to notice the red ants, because it turns and runs away.

I try an experiment, pick up a stiff piece of grass and carefully touch the caterpillar's rear end at the same spot the ant has chosen to attack. What a surprise. The caterpillar makes no response whatsoever, suggesting that it tells the difference between my own peck and the ant's attack. I drop the grass feeling a bit ashamed at myself for trying out a science experiment on a creature in such distress.

BIG THOUGHTS

I'm not very skilled at observing anything quietly for very long without, eventually, letting big thoughts intrude to paint the big picture of what is occurring. Here's my big thought for this particular event.

Until science (and let's not forget the moment the leisure class became the majority and TV appeared in everybody's home), no one thought of communication between species as a matter of predicting gestures, or assigning meaning to sounds or equating sounds with words. No one cared; it was all too intellectual. But before there was John Lilly and Koko the gorilla and double blind experiments and workshops on how to swim with dolphins, there was Aesop, Raven, and Coyote. What was primarily communicated between species was a matter of myth, metaphor, parable, drama. Before there was Martin Luther, Jesus, or Moses, it was the job of our spiritual leaders to sweat over the proper interpretation of the great issues of living, loving, and dying as acted out for our edification by creatures like ants and caterpillars.

I sit in my chair and watch this caterpillar fight for its life. I don't cry. But the personal cloud that has tagged behind me all week long suddenly lifts. Call it interspecies solace.

My rational mind now argues persuasively that this life and death struggle getting played out in the dirt before my eyes must not be hindered. My education tells me not to play God.

But something else begins to affect me far more persuasively. Why should it matter that these are lowly insects? What is this word, *lowly?* It doesn't matter that the caterpillar is a notorious predator of prune plums and that a good shake of the tree would probably produce a minor drizzle of them. If I laid them all next to one another, how long would it take me to identify each one as an individual? What an idea!

Myth does not blossom and bear fruit within the rational mind although, now, it is bursting, full-blown, inside me.

It only seems to matter that I see myself when I look at the caterpillar. And I don't see myself at all when I look, just as intently, at the three ants.

This reflection assures me that I am not neutral. I have taken sides. Maybe my flaw. Maybe my saving grace.

I pick up the caterpillar, stretch it out in my palm, use a fingernail to pry off one ant, and then the other one, drop them to the ground where they immediately start looking around for the next bit of protein to cross their path. Do they remember the caterpillar or is it already like a faraway dream from my own last lifetime.

Placing the caterpillar back in the plum tree seems a little too altruistic. I decide to compromise, so put the caterpillar on a leaf high up on the tarragon plant. I have plenty of tarragon to spare.

LITTLE THOUGHTS

I sit down again, place my hands behind my head, stare at the tarragon plant. Where's the caterpillar? My eyes search for it, branch by branch. Then I spy it. From five feet away my maiden in distress is reduced to an inconsequential green squiggle amidst the pale green finery of the three-foot-tall herb. I have to stand and move closer if I hope to watch the caterpillar cope with its new surroundings.

When I finally leave the scene to answer a ringing telephone, the caterpillar is stretched out to its full length on a leaf.

That was yesterday. I haven't been back to check on it. Other things beckon. It's on its own now.

by JIM NOLLMAN

THE CREATURES ON MY MIND

THE BEETLE

When I stayed for a week in New Orleans, out near Tulane, I had an apartment with a balcony. It wasn't one of those cast-iron-lace showpieces of the French Quarter, but a deep, wood-railed balcony made for sitting outside in privacy, just the kind of place I like. But when I first stepped out on it, the first thing I saw was a huge beetle. It lay on its back directly under the light fixture. I thought it was dead, then saw its legs twitch and twitch again. No doubt it had been attracted by the light the night before, and had flown into it, and damaged itself mortally.

Big insects horrify me. As a child I feared moths and spiders, but adolescence cured me, as if those fears evaporated in the stew of hormones. But I never got enough hormones to make me easy with the large, hard-shelled insects: wood roaches, june bugs, mantises, cicadas. This beetle was a couple of inches long; its abdomen was ribbed, its legs long and jointed; it was dull reddish-brown; it was dying. I felt a little sick seeing it lie there twitching, enough to keep me from sitting out on the balcony that first day.

Next morning, ashamed of my queasiness, I went out with the broom to sweep it away. But it was still twitching its legs and antennae, still dying. With the end of the broom handle I pushed it very gently a little farther towards the corner of the balcony, and then I sat to read and make notes in the wicker chair in the other corner, turned away from the beetle, because its movements drew my eyes. My intense consciousness of it seemed to have something to do with my strangeness in that strange city, New Orleans, and my sense of being on the edge of the tropics, a hot, damp, swarming, fetid, luxuriant existence, as if my unease took the beetle as a visible sign. Why else did I think of it so much? I weighed maybe two thousand times what it weighed, and lived in a perceptual world utterly alien from its world. My feelings were quite out of proportion.

And if I had any courage or common sense, I kept telling myself,

I'd step on the poor damned creature and put it out of its misery. We don't know what a beetle may or may not suffer, but it was, in the proper sense of the word, in agony, and the agony had gone on two nights and two days now. I put on my leather-soled loafers; but then I couldn't step on it. It would crunch, ooze, squirt under my shoe. Could I hit it with the broom handle? No, I couldn't. I have had a cat with leukemia put down, and have stayed with a cat while he died; I think that if I was hungry, if I had reason to, I could kill for food, wring a chicken's neck, as my grandmothers did, with no more guilt and no less fellow-feeling than they. My inability to kill this creature had nothing ethical about it, and no kindness in it. It was mere squeamishness. It was a little rotten place in me, like the soft brown spots in fruit: a sympathy that came not from respect, but from loathing. It was a responsibility that would not act. It was guilt itself.

On the third morning the beetle was motionless, shrunken, dead. I got the broom again and swept it into the gutter of the balcony among dry leaves. And there it still is in the gutter of my mind among dry leaves, a tiny dry husk, a ghost.

THE SPARROW

In the humid New England summer the little cooling plant ran all day, making a deep, loud noise. Around the throbbing machinery was a frame of coarse wire net. I thought the bird was outside that wire net, then I hoped it was, then I wished it was. It was moving back and forth with the regularity of the trapped, the zoo animal that paces twelve feet east and twelve feet west and twelve feet east and twelve feet west, hour after hour; the heartbeat of the prisoner in the cell before the torture; the unending recurrence, the silent, steady panic. Back and forth steadily fluttering between two wooden uprights just above a beam that supported the wire screen: a sparrow, an ordinary sparrow, dusty, scrappy. I've seen sparrows fighting over territory till the feathers fly, and fucking cheerfully on telephone wires, and in winter they gather in trees in crowds like dirty little Christmas ornaments and talk all together like noisy children, chirp, charp, chirp, charp! But this sparrow was alone, and back and forth it went in terrible silence, trapped in wire and fear. What could I do? There was a door to the wire cage, but it was padlocked. I went on. I tell you I felt that bird beat its wings right here, here under my breastbone in the hollow of my heart. I said in my mind, Is it my fault? Did I build the cage? Just because I happened to see it, is it my sparrow? But my heart was low already, and I knew now that I would be down, down like a bird whose wings won't bear it up, a starving bird.

Then on the path I saw the man, one of the campus managers. The bird's fear gave me courage to speak. "I'm so sorry to bother you," I said. "I'm just visiting here at the Librarians Conference, we met the other day in the office. I didn't know what to do, because there's a bird that got into the cooling plant there, inside the screen, and it can't get out." That was enough, too much, but I had to go on. "The noise of the machinery, I think the noise confuses it, and I didn't know what to do. I'm sorry." Why did I apologize? For what?

"Have a look," he said, not smiling not frowning.

He turned and came with me. He saw the bird beating back and forth, back and forth in silence. He unlocked the padlock. He had the key.

The bird didn't see the door open behind it. It kept beating back and forth along the screen. I found a little stick on the path and threw it against the outside of the screen to frighten the bird into breaking its pattern. It went the wrong way, deeper into the cage, towards the machinery. I threw another stick, hard, and the bird veered and then turned and flew out. I watched the open door, I saw it fly.

The man and I closed the door. He locked it. "Be getting on," he said, not smiling not frowning, and went on his way, a manager with a lot on his mind, a hardworking man. But did he have no joy of it? That's what I think about now. Did he have the key, the power to set free, the will to do it, but no joy in doing it? It is his soul I think about now, if that is the word for it, the spirit, that sparrow.

THE GULL

They were winged, all the creatures on my mind.

This one is hard to tell about. It was a seagull. Gulls on Klatsand beach, on any North Pacific shore, are all alike in their two kinds: white adults with black wingtips and yellow bills, and young gulls, adult-sized but with delicately figured brown feathers. They soar and cry, swoop, glide, dive, squabble and grab; they stand in their multitudes at evening in the sunset shallows of the creek mouth before they rise in silence to fly out to sea, where they will sleep the night afloat on waves far out beyond the breakers, like a fleet of small white ships with sails furled and no riding lights. Gulls eat anything, gulls clean the beach, gulls eat dead gulls. There are no individual gulls. They are magnificent flyers, big, clean, strong birds, rapacious, suspicious, fearless. Sometimes as they ride the wind I have seen them as part of the wind and the sea exactly as the foam, the sand, the fog is part of it all, all one, and in such moments of vision I have truly seen the gulls.

But this was one gull, an individual, for it stood alone near the low-tide water's edge with a broken wing. I saw first that the left wing dragged, then saw the naked bone jutting like an ivory knife up from blood-rusted feathers. Something had attacked it, something that could half tear away a wing, maybe a shark when it dove to catch a fish. It stood there. As I came nearer, it saw me. It gave no sign. It did not sidle away, as gulls do when you walk towards them, and then fly if you keep coming on. I stopped. It stood, its flat red feet in the shallow water of a tidal lagoon above the breakers. The tide was on the turn, returning. It stood and waited for the sea.

The idea that worried me was that a dog might find it before the sea did. Dogs roam that long beach. A dog chases gulls, barking and rushing, excited; the gulls fly up in a rush of wings; the dog trots back, maybe a little hangdog, to its owner strolling far down the beach. But a gull that could not fly and the smell of blood would put a dog into a frenzy of barking, lunging, teasing, torturing. I imagined that. My imagination makes me human and makes me a fool, it gives me all the world and exiles me from it. The gull stood waiting for the dog, for the other gulls, for the tide, for what came, living its life completely until death. Its eyes look straight through me, seeing truly, seeing nothing but the sea, the sand, the wind.

by URSULA K. LE GUIN

ORIENTEERING

Between Fairfax and Cataract Falls,
fungus gathers like sleep
and we add it to our life list—
not only the Birds of Point Reyes
or the California Butterflies,
but something under Non-Flowering Plants,
western paraphernalia
that does not fly off
the face of the earth, but remains
minutely immobile, unwilling
to be disturbed like hard rock
beneath the fingers of investigation,
like the center of sex
where gonads secrete their must,
odor of lust, open-veined.
On our local map, things
are missing, like the Kent trail
where mushrooms flourish
and flare beneath the redwoods
and the oaks that love March.
We underestimate our ability
to travel between damp and arid.
Even the red thrust of amanita
pulses through redwood loam.
Every winter the center
of the Marin Water District
defies all the rules of drought
and sprouts—low life, yellow, bold,
finding a home at the roots,
something we miss on the dry side of Tamalpais.
While our hike may take us
into summer, we will miss the wet press of earth
between Kent Lake and the ridge.

by NANCY CHERRY

DESERTS

"Deserts," the poets said, coining on
Green summer swards, "meant drought
Between the red rocks and the dry gulch."
Little did they know of
The wild desert rat or the sly
Saguaro, standing sentinel,
Pointing lean and upturned arms
Toward the sky.

"Wastes and barren hells," they wrote,
Turning their words on sculptured frames of brass
Beaten to the tune of the century's pulse.
Little did they know of
The golden poppy, burning up the sunlight,
Or the barrel cactus nursing its water
Like a miser's gold.
Little did they care
For the venom slung scorpion
Nursing its backbreaking squadrons.

The desert is sly;
It outlives poetry.

by ALAN STUART AUSTIN

WAITING OUT WINTER

Clear and cold as cats' eyes
Idaho nights wring all obscurity
from the skies:
obsidian, ice-light, half a moon.

Bear's had a belly-full—
gone cold and stuporous—
hears only his own dreams.
Smells sow, sweet apples, old meat.

Across the dark valley
dogs in barnyards curl smug, secure
—hounds that shout with half
their hearts.
Coyotes who maimed them with escape,
stop their songs—

to listen stiff-legged for heartbeats of mice.

A thumbnail deep
from breastbone to backbone,
huddled in tunnels of hoarfrost,
still, in the weak blue light.

Small meals at the edge of a galaxy.

by BILL YAKE

ENDANGERED SPECIES

In his windless swamp of alders, deep amid the moss and jonquils,
fleeing from intrepid boggers, hiding where eternal fogs rise;
seeking out the scary spider, such lower types in social status;
crying out his Trans Am window, Buggie boogies through the willows,
exhorting all such lowly friendlies to assemble in Bug Hollow;
to listen up, my waddling toddles, or it's *see ya later* fellows!

So, rackety-ax, co-ax co-ax, who's the first to get the ax?
Chorus? "Not me, not me!" Oh? We'll see. Meanwhile, let's hear it
for the men of Science who in defiance of Mother's nature
interfered with her, and cannot now demur in cool abstention, since
Mother now insists upon the continuing necessity of intervention!

Look. We've seen botanists, biologists, ethologists, geneticists,
evolutionists, zoologists, entomologists, and now ecologists!
And, by wild huckleberry, snail and egret, by now it's no secret
that none of us is yet exempted from the wrath of righteous
"put-it-righters"; so stuff this, precious, in your over-nighter,
and tell me who is truly the endangered species?

Why should any human being pick us for an ad on bumper stickers?
such as: Save the Whale, Majestic Ermine, Whooping Crane and
Balding Eagle. Hug a Hornet would be smarter. Kiss a Cockroach
would be neater! Adopt a Flea and Thrill a Beagle!
And here's a cheer that's really regal!

Fruit fly, gypsy moth, chigger, wasp. Maggot, bedbug, housefly, moth!
Mosquito, bat, rat and mouse! Boll weevil, long-legs, leech and louse!
Let's hear it again for DDT. It hurt people more than you or me!

No, dear friends, they can't even grasp the simplest of reasons for our being, or that we could easily eliminate them in one day or evening. So, just cool it, continue to enjoy and occasionally annoy one—but with the cunningness, acumen of our brothers wasp and asp, until our time comes. Like, dig the sticker on my bomber's bumper: CAUTION, FRIEND! I BRAKE FOR HUMANS!

by RUSS TRAUNSTEIN

PART TWO

NO-LEGGERS OF THE REALLY WILD WEST

TANK THING

The most disgusting living thing I ever saw was growing in the drinking water of my home town. I saw it there because I worked summers in the municipal water department. If you've ever toured a water plant, you know that the water is circulated through large, room-sized tanks filled with various filtering materials, mostly gravels and finer-grain layers. I was just a laborer, and never learned the appropriate terminology for any of this stuff; we just called them the filtering tanks, or the softening beds, and tried to spend as much time as far from them as we could, mostly outside looking for something fun to do, or in the cool, cavernous basement of the building among the gigantic humming pipes, hiding from the bosses during the heat of the day.

But one summer the bosses decided that the softening beds (these were concrete tanks maybe 20 by 20 feet, maybe eight feet deep) needed painting, an arduous process involving scooping out all the filtering material (it looked like sand), scraping the paint down as close to the concrete as we could, and then rolling on a coat of gooey, swimming-pool-green paint. This was a lot more work than we, as summer help, really wanted to do, but once stuck with the job we made the best of it.

The best wasn't very good, however. As our bosses (and everybody else of all ages who worked at the water plant seemed to feel they were our boss) pointed out, the paint was "ether-based." I can't imagine why anyone in any industry composed of grownups would ever choose ether as an important ingredient of something that one normally applies while standing on ladders, but there it was. The stuff was powerful, too; a few snorts and we were well into mental impairment, and our mouths tasted like we'd loaned them out to buzzards for the night. In a great show of occupational responsibility, our bosses wheeled in large floor fans and put them near the doors of the wing of the water plant we were working in, to keep some air moving through. Then, as they hurried away to a safer part of the building, they might lean over the edge of the tank and remind us to take a break now and then—go outside now and then, boys, get a little air.

This was the mood and condition of my encounter. There were three of us that summer: Tom, Greg, and me. We were kind of woozy and thick-headed from the paint, but we still had a collegiate enthusiasm for anything weird, so it was a big event when suddenly Tom, who was scraping or painting or napping under one of the long fiberglass troughs that ran the length of the tank, suddenly announced that we should come and look at what he'd found. As we gathered round, he reached under the trough and flopped this oval-shaped gelatinous thing on top of one of the concrete walls where we could get a look at it. He had noticed it clinging to the underside of the trough.

At first, we were most impressed with its considerable potential for offense; someone immediately observed that you could make your whole family heave at once if you suddenly flopped this thing down on the dinner table. But then, being students who got pretty good grades, our curiosities kicked in and we tried to figure out what it was.

I recall it being perhaps four inches long, a flattened, flexible, slimy, oval disk rather the shape of a clam shell. It was perhaps an inch thick in the middle, and tapered to a fine edge all around. It didn't move or respirate or anything; it just lay there. The upper side seemed to be a sort of bilious putrescent olive color, and the underside was just as repulsive: a pale, a kind of dead-fish gray, but less appetizing. I seem also to recall that it smelled really bad, but I might owe that memory more to the ether than to the thing.

After all the obligatory snot jokes had been made, someone suggested that it might just be a batch of algae, but that proposal was neither fun enough nor adequate explanation for how much like a single "thing" it looked, and how cohesive it was. It took very little poking (that being the amount we were willing to do) to establish that it really held the shape like it was arrived at on purpose, say by evolutionary direction, rather than just happening as some brainless primitive plant glommed onto the trough and grew bigger over the weeks, months, or years.

Then someone proposed that it was a colony of some tiny water creatures that piled up into one big round gob like this for whatever sort of social activity met their taste, but someone else said that no, it was probably one creature, or plant, or whatever, because it was lighter underneath than on top. Looking back, I'm really impressed by this comment (I wish I could claim to have made it, but I just don't remember who did); it suggests that one of us had a knowledge of protective coloration. "Countershading," by which some animals are darker on top and lighter underneath (like a pronghorn, or a trout), is a very useful and common tendency among wildlife, and our Tank Thing apparently was sophisticated enough to evolve this form of camouflage.

So it was probably a single being (though who among us knew if there weren't some tiny creatures who were socially organized enough to bunch together and put all the darker guys on top and the lighter ones underneath?). But how did it get there? We vaguely understood that the water that came into this filtering system emerged from deep wells out behind the plant; perhaps the Tank Thing was just the vanguard of an invasion of Deep Well Things, or Underground River Things. Perhaps it came through the system really small, and grew to its present size (eating something even more disgusting?) in the tank.

It's odd that, as short as our ether-based attention span was at the time, and as quickly as we abandoned our study of the Tank Thing (I don't even remember what we did with it, but I do know Tom was really tempted to take it home to present to his younger sister at some choice moment), I have never forgotten it. It is for me a kind of baseline, against which over the 30 or so intervening years I could measure other supposedly disgusting life forms. I own dozens of field guides, and I've seen nature at its rawest in a lot of parts of North and Central America, but nothing has yet compared, for unbridled willies-generating creepiness, with the Tank Thing.

Come to think of it, maybe it did me a favor. Maybe one reason I'm so hooked on nature at its most willfully gag-inducing and esthetically challenging is because I've already seen the worst. I still gag, I still try to avoid seeing the really bad things, but I'm not surprised that they exist, and I don't mind that they're out there. Something came along at the right time and helped me get over our prissy insistence that nature isn't good unless it's photogenic. Save your slugs and your leeches, your suppurating pustules and your maggoty roadkills; unless you've seen the Tank Thing, nature has been passing you by.

by PAUL SCHULLERY

THE CALIFORNIA FLOATER CLAM

Not very many people living in the Southwest or any other part of this country know much about the California Floater Clam or any other freshwater clam that they may happen upon. No, *National Geographic Magazine* has never published an article about this creature, and I would be surprised if this clam was ever mentioned in that great magazine. This species, *Anodonta californiensis* Lea, was first described back in 1852 from specimens collected from the Colorado River near the town of Yuma, Arizona. Formerly abundant and widespread throughout the western United States, and possibly northwestern Mexico and southwestern Canada, anyone looking for it today would be hard pressed to find a living specimen, except for a few isolated stretches of streams and rivers. All that I have ever seen are a few three-inch-long shells. I have spoken to people who have seen this clam living in relatively undisturbed northern Arizona streams, but its occurrence is quite rare.

What makes this clam so interesting to me is its life history and how its existence affects other aquatic organisms. Fertilized in the female, the larvae, known as glochidia, are released into the water where they sink to the substrate and die or are picked up by fish who stir up the bottom. Parasitic glochidia become attached to the fish, which responds by encasing it in a cyst. After nearly a month of growing under these conditions, the clam detaches from the fish and begins the juvenile stage where it undergoes a two-year transformation to an adult clam.

Juvenile and adult clams feed upon detritus, zooplankton and bacteria, which they convert into biomass and ammonia waste other organisms find useful. Even though I have no evidence, I can imagine River Otters, like their marine relatives on the west coast, finding clams delicious. Perhaps the California Floater Clam made up a part of the River Otter's diet.

Consciously, Americans don't disfavor creatures like the California Floater Clam. The clams don't have any direct effects upon us. This species not living in the lower Salt or Gila Rivers anymore has not contributed to the undermining and collapse of the modern city of Phoenix, Arizona, nor does the absence of this clam influence the production of cotton, lettuce or citrus in the farm fields near Yuma, Arizona. No one went out and tried to eliminate this species like wolves and grizzly bears were in Arizona. I bet there are a few Animal Damage Control officials or livestock growers who have heard of this animal, but no one person or economic interest is guilty. We, meaning all of us who eat vegetables or beef grown in this area or drink water or power our stereos with electricity, have had an effect on this species. We modified parts of the environment for our own purposes with little regard for the effects on other organisms. Through our lack of knowledge and in many cases reckless carelessness, we have disfavored organisms like the California Floater Clam.

The California Floater Clam is rare and has been nominated for protection as an Endangered Species. Unfortunately, not enough information is known about this organism to assign full Endangered Species status. Protecting streams and riparian areas from abuse, such as draining, overgrazing, and pollution, will help keep this species extant and will improve the quality of all life by maintaining a healthy environment for all of us, clams and humans, to live in.

So next time you are wandering along a stream or river, take a few moments to search for the shells of this clam. I have seen them washed up on gravel and sand bars in Chevlon Creek, in northern Arizona, but I am told they can also be found in the White Mountains of eastern Arizona. The bright but delicate mother of pearl that lines the interior reflects a pastel palette of color that will beckon you to pick it up and enjoy its beauty, an enjoyment that was certainly experienced by ancient Hohokam people who collected California Floater Clam shells to fashion jewelry or to just take home to share with someone special.

by THOMAS HULEN

SNAIL POEM

Coming home from a run, I find a snail
not the common garden variety, one
far more exquisite, tortoised, the size of a silver dollar.
I carry it home in the palm of my hand,
my fingers curling around with care.

Along the way, I peek to see if the snail
has pulled its head inside. But it never does.

At home, I go to where my husband sits,
the phone to his ear, newspaper open across his lap,
and present my treasure
setting it down, on today's news.

He moves a little more upright in his seat, grins
before he tells the person on the phone,
his wife just brought him a gift, he has to go.

He watches me play with it, touching the antennae,
coiled shell, as the muscular foot slimes
across the daily columns until, eventually, I take it outside
to the shaded planter.

I am a woman, a lover, a mate
a child. And he
never fails to recognize and embrace each one.

by PAMELA J. PADGETT

THOUGHTS OF A SALMON ON ITS FINAL LEAP

Seen on a Television Commercial

There are important things
they don't tell you
about spawning. Oh, I know
I will blush red,
feel my body grow heavy with desire
to line the pea gravel beds
with rich strings of marbled roe,
how this pleasure
will be enough to make
me die. They don't tell you about throngs
salmon have to swim through
to get there,
about the cataracts
so high and swift
that you may have to accelerate,
hurl your gravid belly
against the current
several times before finally making it.

No one warns you about great bears,
those dark clouds
against a silver sky,
slow arms bristling with rakes
of black lightning to lift you from exhaustion.
I've learned to swim the midstream.
Now I'm accelerating beneath a small fall,
circling,
gaining speed and momentum, up

into the cold, choking freshness of air,
down, down toward a huge
furred rock, a golden brown,
ruffled neck holding out its toothy basket
for a leap so true
it need not even move
its head to catch the flesh dropping
toward grizzly darkness.

by BILL COWEE

THE SWEET FACE OF A SNAKE

I was probably eight, fishing
from a boulder on the bank
of the Walker River like I did
every summer. It was cold
and overcast, I was focused
on the tip of my pole.
Your voice sledged through
the wall of rushing water,
I twisted around, seeing the snake
winding around rocks toward
me, blocking my only exit.
It stopped, seemingly
surveying me with curiosity,
lifting its head and neck
to see what it had found.
I smiled, knowing it only wanted
water, but the urgency of your
voice told me to hold still.
You threw a stone hard
into a nearby bush, its seed
pods rattling like sudden
attack. The snake was gone
before the leaves settled,
and I spent days after
searching for this friend I lost.

by GAYLE SLIVA

BACK TO THE SERPENT

My morning eyes blinked at the wriggle ahead
on the yellow dirt road.
An endorphin popped: bruise it—that flat arrow
head with a red spear inside—under the tires
of my navy blue wagon.

I could have harmed that small smirker, managed
that easily, flattened it quickly,
except for the tail which might have swung back
and forth, out from the tread.

Even the goddess of grassland and swamps would
not stoop to life forms much lower than snakes.
Spiders and roaches have legs, and when pressed
to a spot, or a shrivel, stay there.
Even earthworms, when jabbed, have no bite on the
barb.

I confess, as a youngster sun-free in tall grass, I
captured snakes.
Equipped with white work gloves I lifted them up
from their secret routines—surprised—into white
plastic pails for inspection and forty-eight hour
detention in my house.

These harmless small sins were my relics of home,
of the ancient blood curse, which I felt in my
bones as frozen smooth fear.

While I slept soundly, between the bleached sheets,
a brother of mine, or the merciful father,
would usually grant the snakes pardon,
parole.

My seventh summer I spotted a snake, in brown
grass no more than a strong arm stone's throw
from my family's picnic.
A small, state park snake, out for the eye of the sun
on its back.

I reached down to hold it.
Its fly-catching jaws left a rotten-grass extract that
would not wash off and a spirit slapped down
and dead set against snakes.

After that, when I happened to spot a snake,
resting in apple shade, scooting away from the
lawnmower blade, it turned to me, slithering,
crawled up my arm and down when I shuddered.

I stopped by that snake on the grated dirt road.
In fact I backed up a turn, wanting to loom,
and expecting to see a swift flight or a hot
scripted coiling, down there in the sand.

The slim tube would tremble at my humming
shadow.
I was the tester, the tempter and judge.

But this snake flicked its flag at me, thoughtfully.
Someone had dressed in gold accent, carefully,
gave graceful waves and a permanent flow.
Go nowhere slowly, you're ready to go.

I saw the lines of a whale's diving tail, the whip of
a dolphin's firm motor.
Early sun highlighted muscles and blood pumping
in and out under a casing so fine
that my baby could crush the life, squeezing
a little.

The snake might be thumbing (read: *tonguing*)
trying to tell a stalled driver where slow
moving mice swim in shallow gold pools.
Would I give a hand, lift from the ground to the
front seat, beside me?

I shivered and shifted to low ahead, slow,
careful to turn from the thin smiling face
and the vanishing tail.

by JEFFREY JOHNSON

SNAKE TIME

Sidewinder moves
Its muscles looping criss-cross
from rock to saguaro to sage
through hot sand

Tongue smells yellow-flowered creosote
and fear on an eddy of air

Swallows kangaroo rat
in a sandy squall

Sleeps on warm rose-quartz
and waits for need to move it

Sidewinder moves
Its muscles whipstitch earth to air
Binding all to one
in the unraveling

by RITA A. HOEFLEIN

DIAMONDBACK

Which way did you go today?

I saw your track in the sand.
Wide and curvy,
The soil caressed by your heavy deliberate turns.
Slowly wending your way to a destination.

The trek is considerable after a long winter's nap.

by SUNNIE EMPIE

A KIND OF SEEING

Uncle Walt walked
the old Crook place
blinder than a rock,
swinging a stock cane
with spiteful accuracy
on the old cow
when she crowded
my lugging of the grain.
Or halted me with it
at the waist
  "Watch the wire"
before I felt the metal bite.

Once he hooked me
ass-end over appetite
from a half-stack of bales,
and before my wind was back,
lifted coils
gently from the straw
and slid the diamondback
off into the whispering grass
and to my "Kill it,"
his dusty voice,
"There's worse than snakes."

by WILLIAM SHELDON

RATTLER REBUTTAL

Writhe
rattle and
roll: what
I do. Sure,

my poison
kills. You're human.
Yours kills
as effectively.

When scared
I rattle.
You quiver.
Are we so

different?
You overturn rocks,
spy on fields,
poke your always

open eyes
into any
hiding place.
You eat

or bag me
for churches:
tossing me
proves faith.

I twist
away, bite
when I know
I'm a goner.

by KENNETH POBO

THE BALLAD OF RED TANK DRAW

Single file, we made our way down the rocky cliff.
We'd planned the day to have a look at a favorite petroglyph.
I in the lead, eyes intent, but not expecting any threats,
Rounding a rock I suddenly heard the rattle of castanets!
So I sprang back behind the rock before it was too late,
Drew courage in a moment, and turned to investigate.
That buzzing filled the canyon with a sinister barrage;
Finally I made him out, in his patterned camouflage:
Under the overhang he coiled, the biggest I ever saw:
It was the Rattlesnake Sentinel of Red Tank Draw.

Thorny catclaw on the left, rattlesnake on the right,
the narrow trail went right between, but I could not risk a bite.
That rattlesnake just held his ground—he was not going to shoo,
So from my vantage point I made a plan, I knew what I would do:
I gathered rocks and pitched them in; I made a sort of wall,
Clear to the top of the overhang, about ten inches high, in all.
He could not see, he could not strike, and we were two feet apart
As we hurried past. We were down at last, we saw the fine rock art.
He had the upper hand, all right—though neither hand nor paw
Has the Rattlesnake Guardian of Red Tank Draw.

A couple of hours of food and sun, and then we headed back,
Listening for the rattle that might mean a snake attack.
Staffs in hand, we moved along, and glory be! Yes, sir!
He coiled there, his vibrating tail was nothing but a blur!
Ten feet further down the path, he coiled in a rocky niche,
This cavern too high and wide. We'll choose another route—but which?
First I tried to make him leave; with a husky five-foot staff

I poked his coils; he rose and wove. At first it made us laugh.
Then he opened his jaws, wide and fanged, and we looked down the maw
Of a frustrated rattlesnake in Red Tank Draw.

He hovered and wove above his tail, rattles tickling his chin.
We shrieked and scrambled backwards; we were not going to win.
I retrieved the staff, we paused to search: the only other route
Lay through ten feet of catclaw; it was a painful way to go out!
Once through the thorns, we would emerge right by the barricade
Where rocks enclosed the overhang—the wall that I had made.
The snake was in his cavern now, staked out down below.
As we started across our detour, our progress was pretty slow.
But thorns weren't going to worry us; we'd come within a straw
Of being bitten by the Guardian of Red Tank Draw.

I'd almost cleared the catclaw clump, and guess what met my eye:
That vigorous, vigilant rattlesnake came gli-i-iding by,
Came stealing up the pathway to his homemade lair;
His length was stretched along the trail, full six feet fair!
Stretched along the trail like that, of course he could not strike,
But THREE FEET in front of me was closer than I'd like!
Well, he got behind his barricade, and when the coast seemed clear,
We both dashed past like rabbits, spurred by a thrill of fear.
Once up the cliff like warriors, we gave a loud "Hurrah!"
For the stout-hearted Rattlesnake of Red Tank Draw!

by BEATRICE RICHMOND

RATTLES

Rattlesnakes guard the cemetery
at Rock Creek.
Tumbleweeds sand blast crosses.
Board tombstones with faded names
hold dates too close apart.
I used to fear their venom,
feel the graves alive
with the slither of their sighs.
Now, I hear a benediction
and bone beads whisper
rattled tales of guardians.

by JO NELSON

ON THE WAY TO OJO CALIENTE

Driving up from Santa Fe this afternoon, I watch the sky change: ominous clouds boiling over bright blue. Pink cliffs and grey green pinon, the chamisa thinking in green now, on its way to blonde later in the year.

I think as I am riding along: if I walked up that arroyo and climbed to the top of that mesa, I would smell the thunderstorm coming. See the insects moving faster on the ground in preparation. See the faint shadow of myself, preceding me up the sandy chasm. Wind in the scrub juniper. Somewhere water, but not here and not yet.

Imagine climbing to a quiet ledge and stopping to rest. Sitting cross-legged, I meditate on distant cliffs, fingernail-sized canyons in the distance.

A snake that was a pile of rocks moves slightly, becomes a snake. Rises in sudden alarm at my presence. Invasion of her spot. I, seeing the snake, feel my own stomach coil in fear. Nothing moves, however. I sit still and the snake stays in its loose coil, head up, staring.

My mind runs rapidly through all the possibilities, the various things I could do. It selects the last one: sitting still and thinking good thoughts about the snake. So I do. I slow my breathing and in my heart begin to make good poems for the snake.

> Snake, O living line
> S upon the mesa pink
> I think
> You are divine
> Snake your home is sweet
> Dry and airy
> Thank you for having me
> To afternoon prayers

and so on. I beam good energy to the snake. Still in loose coil. Head raised: I can see it weaving out of the corner of my eye. She could strike. Lightning could also strike me here on this cliff perch. But neither happens. As I relax, the snake drops slowly to the ground and flows smoothly forward over the sandstone ledge towards me.

Breathing is so important.

The snake is coming at me, but not to hurt me. To investigate. My hands are cradled together in the cup of my crossed legs. Breathing is everything. Breathe in and send warm vibes to the huge beautiful diamondback rattler who is wavering at my left knee.

I'm not making it up.

It's happening.

The snake, it is a "she," I can feel it. She glides up into my lap slowly, dragging the indescribably long weight of herself across my left knee, left wrist, hand finger knot, right wrist, right thigh. And stops. Pauses. Her metallic bone-like flesh-like skin is cool on my wrists. Pulsating.

I breathe as fast as a train in my mind's eye, but I know I am holding on to the last one.

Am I safe?

Yes of course—comes a voice that is not my own.

Not in words I form a question that repeats that thought—with my breath? My mind?

The voice says: I won't hurt you.

The snake drops her head and glides slowly off the edge of my right leg, sticking close to my body. She moves around me, encircles me. Her head appears again at my left knee before her surreal pyramid of opaque rattles even clears the path. She pauses. Her tail crosses my wrists. The rattles are warmer than the rest of her skin.

I stare at the pink mesa in the distance. Blue black thunderclouds mass over it. The light is an eerie, misunderstood kind of yellow.

Don't be afraid, says the voice. And I realize that the snake is talking to me. Encircling me.

by M. CORBIN GOULD

RATTLESNAKE HAIKU

The rattlesnake's head—
a tool for sifting troubles,
a wedge for the sand.

The rattlesnake's gut—
a long trip on her belly,
a short road for mice.

The rattlesnake's tail—
a stack of successful skins,
a queenly display.

by JEN BLACKHORSE

PART THREE

TWO-LEGGERS OF THE REALLY WILD WEST

THE BAT FROM BURLEY

The bat
Must have clung
To the canvas
Back of the old
Blue El Camino
Fifty miles
Through the dark
Snake roads
of desert Idaho

In the morning
The batlet
Brushed my neck
As we unloaded wood
To daylight sonar

The sound of wings
Caught our breath
But the dark flyer
Was already
In the ice palace sky
And flew into the woods
Near the river

by TONY D'ARPINO

TWILIGHT APPOINTMENT

I must hurry.   The day colors
drain the skies
and I have an appointment to keep.

A cool air   heavy
with musty memories of marsh
reaches out.   The boat rocks madly
in my hasty escape—but then finds itself.
Rushing my oars, I position myself precisely
upon the dark patterned waters   and wait.

There—just above the surface,
my eyes strain to focus.   Did I imagine it?
In a Stealth approach, skimming low, flying fast,
but dead-on target
      come
my old friends—the bats.

I like to think
they play a game of chicken
with the boat and me, to see
if I have gained courage.
They streak past me, afterburners glowing,
their foxy little grins firmly in place.
Proving air superiority over pesky mosquitoes
that dance in my heat, the bats win;
I blink.

An oar creaks.
The Will of the night breeze
catches the boat
and it   slowly   turns.   My sight drops
to view the water's moon
break into shimmering pieces.
It is late.

Regretfully, I turn the boat,
and prepare for reentry
among those who call a cabin
—safe—and home.

by LAURA SNYDER

BORNE THROUGH THE AIR

Night's bat is my fate, we share what we must:
Lightly made, I am grace that grew flimsy;
In the wrong environment I break.

I can fly, though not well when near the light
Of industrial civilization's craving flame.
I live deep in the earth; an inheritance
Of excrement piles up below me,

Potent, rich, ready for the fields of theocracy.
Misunderstood always, often feared or hated
For nothing, for nothing, I communicate best
By radar.

I have an appetite for insects; I take them
By surprise, eat them, insects
Or anything that flies like it was crawling.

by THOMAS WHITEHEAD

WHY I WATCH SPARROWS

Because they are ordinary.
Because they are everywhere.
Because they have to scrabble each day for food.
Because they are not flashy.
Because they are intent on their business.
Because they are adapted to their lives.
Because they do nothing extraordinary.
Because they get shoved about by squirrels.
Because they are mentioned in the Bible.
Because they depend on Earth.
Because they stay for the Winter.
Because they stay for the Summer.
Because they look out for each other.
Because they follow their rules.
Because of their diminutive size.
Because they make precise movements.
Because they can land on a chain link fence.
Because they can land in a chain link fence.
Because they are mentioned in Zen Koans.
Because they can pick up a grain at a time with their beaks.
Because they are always vigilant.
Because they are not gaudy.
Because they can peck at the ground without mashing their beaks.
Because they can land on a stem of grass.
Because they are always busy with something.
Because they don't sit around and think about it.
Because they live inside their lives.
Because they appear to understand their lives.
Because they are inscrutable to us.
Because they are not inscrutable to themselves.
Because they hop to walk.
Because they give each other space.

Because they form patterns when they peck at the grain.
Because they learn to trust humans.
Because they live around us.
Because they are written about by Dr. Williams.
Because my mother hates them.
Because they have life.
Because they hang together.
Because they puff up their feathers in the cold.
Because they remind me of water.
Because I have to feed them.
Because they are afraid of us.
Because they jump up at a noise.
Because they fly in patterns.
Because they watch in patterns.
Because of the precise movements of their heads.
Because I shot one with a BB gun when I was a kid.
Because I shot them with a .22 a few years later.
Because ammunition companies make .22 shells called bird shot to
kill them.
Because the shells are crimped golden and beautiful.
Because they are mentioned in the Koran.
Because I never got any thrill out of killing them.
Because many people consider them to be pests.
Because they flew in the Quonsets where the tractor was parked.
Because they built their nests in the corners of the Quonsets.
Because their nests were built of twigs and bits of string.
Because they fly up all at once.
Because they are of one mind.
Because they have a simple order.
Because they have built no cities.
Because they have worn no clothes.
Because they have started no wars.

Because they have outlived Caesar in all his robes.
Because they outlive Hitler in all his hate.
Because they don't believe in politics.
Because they keep focused on the real.
Because they have no illusions.
Because they are not trying to change the world.
Because they fit in.
Because they give back.
Because they seem very stern but must be gentle in their hearts.
Because I can guess all these things about them.
Because they do not pay attention to me except when they are hungry.
Because they are destined to be some of the last creatures.
Because they think for themselves.
Because so many other birds are gone from our lives.
Because the frogs and toads are disappearing.
Because they have not ceased to be.
Because they live wrapped in the meanings of their lives.
Because they have witnessed everything.

by GREG KOSMICKI

STARLINGS

Hundreds of starlings have landed
in the trees across the street.
It is the time of year
when they do this. This is the
tree they have on their maps
at which they never look.
Hundreds of starlings have landed in the trees
and they are making their music
which many people
hate it is so ugly
it does not roll on the ear
like the Robins' or Meadowlarks'
it does not mean what is in our hearts.
But it is one of the meanings of mine.
Hundreds of these birds are singing
they even made the buzz saws a little muter
although they are persistent
they are going to cut something
down that is their job
which like all objects
the function is in the form
since you do not see
any pottery objects
cutting off tree limbs,
butchering up the old elms.
Hundreds of birds in the trees
and the world is almost
ended
they have taken it all
from us, from the birds
from the cattle
from the fish and snapdragons.

Hundreds of birds in the trees
singing here I am
here we are
this is our tree
a while this is our
earth take us
since you will
for now we sing
as we know how to sing.

by GREG KOSMICKI

JAY JOY

Steller's jay is back,
shaking his shiny black crest,

climbing the fir tree branch by branch,
past the confident crow,

all the way to the radiant crown—
where he leaps in pure blue light.

by JANINE CANAN

QUOTH THE CORVID

Before dawn departs from canyon walls,
the forest fills with ravens' calls.
But closer down in my backyard
flies a smaller, louder, bright blue bard.
His swooping flight from scrub to tree,
from branch to ground, from ground to me
leads him to my window's edge
from where he calls friends to his ledge;
bursts of beaky, creaky, shrieking screams
lift the sleep that holds my dreams.

Jay, smallest of the family Corvid,
sounds as if he's from the core of id.
Like cousins raven, magpie, and crow,
the size of jay's voice is his main show.
For loudness, my blue-winged buddy is not to blame;
he just tries to live up to the family name.
Forgiving him, I look into those beady eyes
and know that it is time to rise.
He glares back, giving me that sideways glance,
neck stretched forward, voice enhanced.

If quoth the raven, "Nevermore,"
then quoth the scrub jay, "Furthermore
and furthermore ..."

by ADRIENNE ZAMORE

THE DAY OF THE CROWS

Yesterday my world was full of doves.
Today it's full of crows.
All other birds have disappeared.

I like these brash adventurers so blackly elegant,
so harshly eloquent in shouted conversation from palm
to deodar.
What can this discussion be?
        Politics?
        Sermons?
Or are they simply telling jokes,
topping one another,
splitting the sky with raucous laughter?
No matter.
At last they all take wing, move on.

Immediately a multitude of sparrows clamor
in the magnolia tree.
A flick of movement is a linnet in the hedge
and two doves fly across my vision's edge.

by RUTH ADAMS

POGROM IN A COMMUNITY GARDEN

Bill Gopher's Bane is angry with me.
Very well.
He switched from killing gophers
to assassinating crows.

During the gopher wars he used to come
all down the garden
to my thirty square feet of peace
to display his latest mangled trophy and to boast
the sickening tally of his victories thus far.
"Thirty-six," he'd say,
"This makes thirty-six this month!"

The crows came—
aeronautical pirates
flaunting black flags in the summer breeze.
It took real strategy to beat them to the strawberries.

By the community compost heap
a tall post appeared, Bill's trap a-dangle.
He has retired it for the season, I supposed,
and thought, a good hard blow now with a rock . . .
but stayed my hand.

So I was grubbing weeds
when wild hysteria erupted in the crow community.
Outside the fence an old man passing, stopped.
Together we peered down the rows of burgeoning green
at mad black fluttering.
"Come," said Old Man, "Let me in. We'll set him free."

At our approach the flock retreated.
Except for two: one who hovered, screaming,
and one gripped fast,

its bleeding foot between the jaws of Bill's cruel trap.
Old Man swore softly.
Then he caught the struggling bird,
held it still while I released the trap.

We watched it spring into the air
and greet its anxious mate.
But as they flew away,
a foot, bitten through the bone, fell off.
"He'll be all right," Old Man consoled,
"They're tough. But who would do a thing like that?
They don't take much."
The trap lay in my hand.
I grabbed a rock and smashed it flat.
"That one will never kill again.
I should have done this long ago."

Bill Gopher's Bane came raging down the garden rows.
"Someone's broke my best trap!
I already got a couple o' them crows.
But now someone's broke my trap!"

I grinned. "Too bad."

He glared. "They'll get your corn for sure.
I seen them strip a field in nothing flat!"

The crows are gone now.
I haven't seen them since that day.
Only in memory I see the two black shapes
huddled close together in a palm.

Bill hasn't spoken to me since.

by RUTH ADAMS

MAGPIE

Magpie wears tails
& eats leftovers.
Daughter of crow
& owl of Albion.
Dreams on black haw
in the shadow of the moon;
pale owl, fully eclipsed;
old crow at noon.
Magpie holds tight to her carrion
before licking her black talons
clean with her shrewd tongue.
She pulls her shattered brother
from the incision,
the black interstate.
She is both sides
of the Tao. She is hungry.
Logicians are her enemies.
She makes her own nonsense
from plentiful incongruities.

by BILL YAKE

In the distance a metallic-black raven
rides the thermals over Grand Canyon.
Silently he tips to the left, to the right,
soaring and dipping, suspending time.
He does not move wings, head or tail
    but hovers like a dark shadow-
    self above the vast, empty space.

by MARY WILLETTE HUGHES

 VULTURES

Black leaves
butterfly shadows
flakes of ash
spiraling on updrafts
lifting toward the sun

Dark knights
in blood red hoods

Earth angels

I should lie down for you
on crossbedded sandstone
and spread my own
arms wide

by ANN WEILER WALKA

VULTURES PEACOCKS KALI MA

From the frothy boas of their Machiavel ruffs
pop the sore red privates of the vultures' heads
startling the timid, the polite and the pretty

Benign and unconcerned, their day's work done
the vultures wheel and float in the weakening sun
roost in the tallest tree of Tombstone Canyon

From below scream the peacocks up at them,
"You dirty death eaters
You ones without mirrors
Go drop your dark feathers on somebody else."

And the vultures, incredulous
rest in the tree
having spent all day perfuming the canyon
having tended the ones that life abandoned
asking . . .

"Have you never in yourselves
seen succulent darkness
the Mother's complexion,
her blue black sheen?

Have you maybe supposed
you are different from the rest
and do not take your milk from the Corpse's breast?"

by PATRICIA CATTO

MUDHEN

There's something about
the American Coot, that
causes one to snort . . .
to hoot.

With a silly waddle
like a seasick duck,
I watch in wonder
from my beat-up truck.

He swims so freely
'tween river and bay,
leaves four-toed tracks
outlined in clay.

The Paiute proclaim,
"He tastes like chickens."
Offer me some, I'll
run like the dickens.

So before I go
and it's too late,
I simply wish to
reiterate,

there's something about
the American Coot, that
causes one to think . . .
not shoot.

by MICHAEL KIRILUK

UNTITLED

on highway
two thirteen
this morning
i saw an eagle
on a speed sign
and had to
stop

idle ‘cycle
humming
i felt frail
beneath my leather

white head cocked
to the side
sizing me up
with a
black quarter eye
sun gleams
off scaled talons

upon
wings wider
than my highway
it sauntered
into the sky

by SAM BARASCH

PART FOUR

FOUR-LEGGERS OF THE REALLY WILD WEST

RAIN, LOVE, AND SPADEFOOT TOADS

Driving from Los Angeles toward Palmdale on Highway 14 you will pass the town of Acton that, in the middle of the '70s, was a good deal smaller than it is now. Homes and businesses hadn't sprouted up like mushrooms after rain. The wide, sparsely populated, toast-colored valley slopes away to your right and ends at the mouth of Soledad Canyon. The foothills surrounding it on three sides are worn, ancient and charred by the glare of the sun. Your eyes are relieved only by the occasional green of eucalyptus or elm trees, carefully tended by those long forgotten to this valley.

One spring is especially memorable. We were deluged by hard-driven rain that never let up for days on end . . . 23 long days. It poured day and night, and we began to believe it would never stop. We were under a huge pot lid of aluminum-colored sky that seemed to stretch forever.

There was a swimming pool whose bottom was cracked to the rear of our house. I looked out in disbelief one morning, through rain-sheeted windows, to see that it was full of water. The rain had soaked the desert so abundantly that the water had risen through the crack and sought its level, threatening to overflow. The dry wash that was Soledad Creek, where we hunted agates, walked the dogs, and let our desert tortoise graze, flash-flooded to become a wicked, brown torrent that created a river of destruction. It took life and property and weeks to subside.

But sweetly and secretively, the western spadefoot toads (*Scaphiopus hammondi*) knew that this was the time for love. Out of their deep burrows they emerged from a state of estivation which had kept them safe for a year. I am sure that all of Acton's spadefoot toads made their way to the quiet water of our swimming pool, forsaking the creek, to sing their lusty mating songs, to breed and spawn their strings of eggs. The nights were made for toad love, and we fell asleep to their testosterone-charged trilling.

Spadefoot toad eggs hatch in two days, but more toads had joined the group and our pool was full of toads of all ages—from the newly hatched to adults. The rain finally stopped, and very slowly the water in the pool began to drain back through the crack. The receding water was black with toads. Thousands of spadefoots, hopping, swimming, eating (each other, for they are carnivorous). We knew if we left them they would die, and so began the family rescue effort. We scooped them into buckets for days and moved them to safety until they were all gone, tadpoles to the gentling water of Soledad Creek and adults to the safety of the empty fields around the house.

Our German Shorthair Pointer, Fancy, never learned that toads were not to be picked up, for they tasted terrible and made her foam at the mouth.

Most people travel through the desert on the way to somewhere else. For long, boring miles the desert rests quiet and somnolent. So much is missed. It is a land of great mystery and it teems with life. You cannot live on the desert. You must live with it a while to understand the throbbing multitudes of life it holds close to its heart.

The spadefoot toads are a stellar example of the desert's secrets. Every time I see a toad, no matter where I am, I remember 23 days of unusual desert rain and a swimming pool alive with remarkable spadefoot toads.

by MAY L. LENZER

HELIOPHILIA

Horned Toad
perched on flatrock
turns an eye toward western sky
the desert sun
and, like an ancient priest
worships that great orb.

by G. L. PETTIGREW

❋ OUR SHOCKINGLY DIRTY GARDEN

I want to come back to that garden with the toad
in it. For us, both of them are real.
The garden's gone wild, shocking disarray,
weed-choked, dry, chockablock with cactus and scrub.
We look out our dust-streaked window and think,
"What's the use? This is nature taking over
the effort to impose order."
The horned toad is perfectly hidden sitting in dirt.
We have to be looking exactly at him to catch
his placement in this scene.
He knows he's not toad at all, but lizard
with hornlike spines. Clever fellow to hide out
on earth in full view. His life is insects,
catching them for food, keeping his own kind
of order in the yard.

It's hot. Wind stirs the dirt, but the toad
stays put.

by LAUREL SPEER

THE ALLIES

Alone in the garden, I think:
knees in the dirt, sun hot on my back.
Only the weeding tool moves,
bites deep beneath my urging hands.

Suddenly a flick of motion:
a fleeing to a sheltering cabbage leaf.
I see you there, minute descendent of Tyrannosaurus Rex,
frozen into stillness,
the dusty complications of your hide matching the soil,
your bright eye cocked upon me.

You need not fear for we are allies you and I.
Together we tend this garden earth,
mutual legatees of all that came before
when your kin ruled the steaming swamps.

Peace be between us.
When I withdraw, this makeshift Eden will remain
all yours.

by RUTH ADAMS

❋ MY SISTER THE GILA MONSTER

All I own sways behind
in that orange U-Haul
wobbling across Arizona,
my Dodge to the desert.

Filming those geriatric
infomercials was dull,
Dallas a dry cow skull.
Now I'm elated lizards

love in cactus heaven,
squat body no monster.
Cute as the Mona Lisa,
their snouts doze from

9 to 5; citron tongues
tip the moon. I brake
at the next arroyo, set
to meet my new sisters.

by EDWARD C. LYNSKEY

NABHAN—CLAN OF THE LIZARD

for the Family of Gary Paul Nabhan

Lariat-noosed by small hands,
  fourteen loosed lizards
bask in a dry porcelain tub.
  Spinies, Collareds, Trees, and Whiptails,
lassoed to make their acquaintance—Howdy!

Learned lizards lure our feet
  to stalk stillness in canyon walls.
Lizards drop and draw the loop,
  pull us close, to see our eyes.
They weave of us a family story
  bound tight with knots to lizard lore.

by LAURA SNYDER

THE ACCUSATION

Arizona alligator
spotted belly crawler
pink-tongued licker

part-time body climber
live-bearing
scorpion snacker

secretive
Sierra Madre to Jalisco
rock slider

desert dancing
slick suited
toenail clicker

You
think life is a
sunstroked orgy.

by NORAH BOOTH

If I'm gone from the cabin too long
mice move in and claim a spot, soft & dark
scurrying right past the electronic device
that chirps, Go back! Go back!

Droppings trail from room to room
I run their maze, well-trained in hide & seek,
and find they've birthed among my socks
which now reek of pee & poop
and must all be washed

(Last year they discovered Kotex
made a cozy nest, glycerin soap
a special treat)

When I draw back the quilt and see
one turd centered just so
atop my yellow pillow case, I shriek
and nominate these vermin
for the Endangered List

But their trick with the soup ladle
finally makes me laugh, and recant:
I don't know how they shimmy down
the slippery shaft, sniff, then turn
heinie in and shit just one

Into the ladle's cup, but I love
their concept of sport!

by MEREDITH SABINI

❁ ENCOUNTER WITH A DEER MOUSE

What moves this morsel of the night,
to creep into my candlelight?
It starts and sniffs, betraying fear,
then lingers still, and still is near.
Perhaps, like moths, it feels from flame,
a primal pull devoid of name.
Perhaps, like me, it longs for day,
and seeks a wayward, feeble ray.

by MATT RASMUSSEN

RAT RAP

Rats carry themselves
with dignity.
Full of panache,
they sneak into
impossible places—

our saints strain
toward impossible places,
especially heaven.
Even with prayer,
we're pretty clumsy.

Not so the rat
who darts and slips
in effortlessly. We
revile them for making
a home from trash,
feasting on discards.

In Vegas I saw
rats behind
a big casino,
hungry and efficient,
wasting nothing. Inside

the casino people
gnawed themselves
before slots
and tables, spinning
wheel saints.
Like rats, they
were also trapped.

by KENNETH POBO

ALL DAY THE RACCOON

who climbed the wrong tree
at the wrong season—
the specifics:

still winter despite
a surprising celsius surge
to shirtsleeves weather,

the tree a skinny Alberta maple
tree surgeons trimmed too well,
had it leaves, they'd not hide a bird,

and the raccoon: skinny too,
unaccustomed to light or warmth,
but recalling last fall's garbage cans—

was caught out at sunrise curled
like a coonskin cap in the crotch
of a tree too scrawny to hide him.

Not expecting hibernation to end
so soon, any more than we did,
like us, he looks sleepy, befuddled,

concerned by the dozen certified breeds
barking beneath him, churning
the thawing beige lawn into mud,

not too involved with each other,
their elation over our untimely spring,
to notice him overhead.

The raccoon may only pretend
to disregard the noisy
messy world 20 feet down.

He may not be awake enough
to remember: even dogs
finally get called home.

Since descent is risky
and the sun uncommonly warm,
and more snow is due soon

forcing return to quiescence,
for now he stays hunched on his perch.
I maintain my parallel watch.

by ELISAVIETTA RITCHIE

ARMADILLO

(from *Earth Elegance*)

You put up the prehistoric
fight of fights,
thanks to
your small and
easy-to-tuck-away size,
thanks to those
soul-shaped tongues
as strong as will,
your armor,
raging battles in your behalf
against a harsh, changing and
creature-crowded tropic,
today, the dusty tumbleweed
plain called panhandle.

Here, only snake, coyote,
owl and roadrunner keep you company
under a moon cradled crescent
like a DNA spiral
on permanent vacation,
while your other brothers
evolved new planets,
curled into balls
in nooks of rainforests
in that continent south.

Up north, even armadillos
walk tall and proud in the sun
like the native Texans they are,
perhaps you were the first ones
with wide, bony plates

like 10-gallon solar panels,
even if your rhythmic steps are on tiptoe,
your babies scurrying
like wind-up toys
to fool those desert campers,
with wizened leather faces,
peering bleary-eyed from tents,
for another
million years.

by CYNTHIA GALLAHER

FOX ON TEMPLE PATH

Tanuki watches me in
alder grove. Nothing
on her mind but hunger,
belly full of new life.

Show her my hands
empty, try to send her
away but she waits to speak
of motherhood, birthing
feeding her young.

I like her philosophy
open and frank.
Poverty is pure.
She says what she has to
without complaint.

Tail whisks a high-pitched
cicada. Sun dapples red fur.
Bell rings in the tower.
She shrugs, turns on
the upward path, treasures
curled in her middle.

Calm and elegant
she never looks back.

by EIDO FRANCES CARNEY

❊ FULL MOON AND FOX

The fox at the edge of woods smells chicken.
As his eyes watch us tear white meat
with teeth, September sun sets and full moon
appears above Tamalpais where the world
is upside-down and we stand on cloud.

The fox, silent below oak and pine, twitches
across an invisible line. He hesitates.
As moon and fox hover, we discard our bones,
climb cold serpentine and, with clouds
shrouding feet, begin to bay at the brightness.

The fox sees day-for-night, mimics a dog
when he flicks his white-tipped tail.
Again we howl. Wildness gorges us, shivers
our throats. In the wind, our noses pinch,
ears sharpen, hackles rise on scalps and across

our backs. We see nothing but moon and sky,
hear nothing but mingled voices, smell nothing
but musk, a momentary rankness. We are
weightless, have lost our bones. From another
peak, we hear faint answers to our cries.

by SUSAN TERRIS

❁ MY BROTHER THE JAVELINA

Nights I jockey a Peterbilt across
the Texas panhandle, my bones an implosion
of weary woe, cantaloupes by the ton
mellowing in refrigeration, any company
is much welcome. Other truckers
over strong black coffee tell me how
DeSoto's conquistadors on mustang
ponies often appear over starlit scrub.
Minds can go awry it seems anywhere
alone along this naked Interstate.
But I count myself among the sane.
And living. Slowing en route to Taos
that eerie hour ghosts stir up a fuss,
I scan the storm-gutted arroyos,
catching amber orbs, meerschaum tusks,
bristled ruffs. Cab window down, elbow
hanging out, I let out championship
hogcalls. Once husky squeals skirr back,
I relax—it's my brother the javelina.

by EDWARD C. LYNSKEY

A MESSAGE FROM JAVELINA BROTHERS

(from *Earthwalker*)

Messages come in many forms as I walk upon this earth. The river or sky can speak of things, or a javelina can talk to you. A storm can destroy your home or the water and wind can rush over your life, setting you free. It's all in what you hear.

I walked over the singing hills with my dog-friends one day. After a few miles I sat down by some bushes overlooking a cattle pond to listen to the earth for a while. Often you do not know what is within you until someone or something talks to you. Well, the javelinas wandered over to speak, huffing and snorting, since my one half-breed Chow dog, Ding, had invited them out. He had circled their nest that was hidden but a dozen yards away, bark-talking to them. My insides were full of fear that day as the javelina charged out, a song, a message on their thin bristly lips.

I took off running out over the hills, the dogs in a circle out to the horizon. The javelina, however, stayed close by my side; snuffling, they trotted close enough so I could feel their prickly breath on my legs, admire the bone-white teeth and worn earth-colored digging tusks. Their wrinkling, wet noses looked like the ends of elephants' trunks, and, looking in their deep-set, near-sighted eyes, I saw the two-legged I was. As I ran and walk-trotted, my fear flowed out of me, scattering across the hills on the wind.

After a mile and a half I was sufficiently tired to slow down and listen. "Hello, two-legged," the javelina said, wiggling their noses and ears.

"Glad to meet you, javelina brothers," I answered, at last getting the message. I was enjoying the running, the edge of excitement in setting free my fear. The sun was setting, chuckling over how hard it is to get Grace Deer to run. The dogs gathered back around, smiling, and the javelina, grunting, sprinted off.

I was going to say they went home, but they were home. The

whole of earth was their house, roof of sky, music of wind, beds of grass. And for that brief moment, as they trotted off, I was reminded I was home, too. Wind stroked my tangled hair, the earth massaged my feet as I walked over her, feeling the message at last.

by GRACE DEER

JAVELINA SUNRISE

In the spring of 1980, a group of animals I had given little previous thought to made a dramatic entrance into my world. I had spent two serene and uneventful nights camped on a ridge high in the Rincon Mountains. Life soon would become extraordinary in its ordinariness.

In the bright, early hours of the morning I began to prepare to regretfully return to the bustle of Tucson. I began to roll and tie my sleeping bag when I heard an odd shuffling and snuffling. I couldn't imagine—oh, an animal! A javelina; it didn't see me, just kept walking, rooting and chewing, no more than twenty feet away. I stepped back, uncertain as to whether I was in any danger. (I had heard that the peccary could bite viciously when cornered.) The rooting, grunting noises became louder. I stood transfixed. Two, three, four, five, six, seven! I became aware that there were javelina on the other side as well, not paying me any mind at all. I stamped my feet. They startled for an instant, then continued their slow, chewing ascent.

An entire band engulfed me. I didn't know whether to panic and run, try to shimmy up the nearest saguaro, or to introduce myself. Most of the javelina were as large as medium-sized dogs; some were a little larger than others. There were a few small ones—a couple followed one of larger size that I presumed to be their mother.

Twenty-seven, twenty-eight, twenty-nine . . . bringing up the rear was the largest javelina by far of the band, no doubt the dominant animal. It was alert, cautious, and definitely aware of me, whether by sight or scent. I could feel the raw power in its patient glare. I stood frozen, picturing myself as a wild pigs' picnic. A minute passed. Tension filled my body. I reached for a rock, growled and lunged forward a little, not knowing what I was risking or if I was risking anything. The large peccary stood its ground. Another minute passed. Satisfied at what it saw or sensed, it slowly turned and followed its band, a handful of stragglers following behind. I had counted thirty-four javelina!

I finished tying my bedroll, then started down the mountain and onto the valley floor. The javelina had left a clear trail for me to follow. They had wound their way systematically up a rugged, trailless hillside, grazing as they went. They didn't seem to linger long enough to consume entire stands of prickly pear or shrubs; the clusters of cactus and catsclaw were nibbled on and wisely left to survive.

I returned to the noise and congestion of my human habitat uplifted by this encounter. I will always thank the javelina for sharing with me a glimpse of their desert, a world that is inexorably vanishing. Surely these animals walk in beauty.

by KATE ROBINSON

NATURE LOVER

Little apples
Sunlight dapples.
Perfect cover
For a lover.

Lovely quiet,
I will try it.
Brush can screen a
Javelina.
Something rank
At the tank.
Trampled edges
Of the sedges.
Cloven hooves
Making moves
In the night mud
Of a light flood.
Juniper checkery
Hiding peccary.
Black and white hair
Just over there.
Overturned root
So near my boot.
Prickly pear rent,
All passion spent.

If I had more time today
Beasts would surely come my way.

Just a chance
Of happenstance.
As it is,
I'll just glean
Evidence of things unseen.
Total stillness
Feels like illness.
Patience gone,
I'll move on.

But if I came here everyday,
Beasts would surely pass my way.

Little apples
Sunlight dapples.
Perfect cover
For a lover.

by MELANIE LEFEVER

BOBCAT

Coming down from the mountain we saw him
coming down from the mountain he ran

Like ink into the brush, spotted, long-legged bobcat
with the split-pause of listening to the mountain

Lost in fog, wildflowers stripped of color—thrift
dull as nickels, and the dandelions face down,

Not even close to seed. Though it is May, the weather
betrays us. We wait for sun on the mountain

And get gray instead; the bay below, a fold of flesh
like my own arm turned toward the body. Coming down

On a Monday, the Brewer's blackbirds and quail
walk their way into view, each turn an agitation of birds,

Each turn a slowing into their wing-world. Sparrows
nip at the berm, crows strut up and back, here

The bobcat, caught at a walk, then a lope and look
over his shoulder at whatever's coming down

The mountain, unexpected, this rumor of the wild
walking into a turn, a bobcat young as the lupine

Waving their blue-white heads, his cat-reach
long as a spider that can peel and leap from rock

To outcrop, lisp of leg that corners a block of web, shortcut
the cat takes, silent passage from manzanita to oak.

We look down the mountain and cannot recognize
anything but chaparral: greasewood,

Elderberry, scrub and red-tipped leaves signaling
spring. Among these shades, the cat disappears

To our delight. We never expected him, never came
so close—tail a twitch of wander, legs, long and singing

Like this trail—quick in a turn of annoyance or curiosity,
even hurry, he takes to the bracken and silence takes the cat.

by NANCY CHERRY

ENCOUNTER

Mountain lion stretched then folded down
to rest within his pollen-colored coat

He tucks limbs tightly in like luggage
leaving out the sicklemoons that end his meaty paws

His tail's a flicking metronome that guides the running creek
his eyes hold black parentheses in case I dare to speak

He licks at August air through a split lip lined in ribbon
the canyon walls and ridges are swallowed in his yawn

The scar on his flank is a leather diamond
scraped furless shiny wilderness brand

by BINNIE PASQUIER

❁ ANIMAL INSTINCT

They hunted down a mountain
Lion today after
It had killed a human intruding
In its domain
Killed it as an example
Though it's hard to fathom
How other animals will
Get the message
To stay away from humans
Which for centuries they
Have tried to do

by A. D. WINANS

COYOTE DANCER

Late June in the Sierra Nevada Mountains of California, the snow was still hiding in pockets of shadow above timberline. The belly flowers were in bloom; tiny bursts of color and intricate form you walked on and over and didn't see until you put your face on their level. The smallest of miracles, miracles nevertheless.

We were travelling to Caples Lake—eagerly anticipating cold nights, high country sunburn and altitude sickness to spend time fishing and exploring the rugged alpine spine of our state. This morning was bright and clean. The pine needles glowed as if polished. Rays from the rising sun poked fingers of pure light through the still misty pine forest. The road was a ribbon twining through the granite rubble of ancient glacial movement and we were alone. Or so we thought.

Something caught our eye.

In a tiny meadow at the edge of the forest, a coyote danced. The guard hairs in its coat were backlit by sunbeams, and the animal danced in an aura of gold.

A coyote dancing? Perhaps not. Reason tells me that he was catching his breakfast. Voles, moles, meadow mice, ground squirrels, chipmunks, and other rodents abound in the Sierra meadows. But still, his dance was a study in grace and sinuous acrobatics: A leap to clear the grass; a pounce; a toss of the head and a wriggle of the hips. A crouch, a bound. Ageless choreography—the whole program repeated. At each movement dew flew from the grasses into the air around him, glittering in sprays of silver droplets.

We slowed but didn't stop. He never noticed us.

He was a study in freedom and beauty, the essence of wildness, of nature left to its own devices. Perfection.

In the whole universe, at that precise moment in the early morning light, on a date lost in time, how lucky we were to see a coyote dance.

by MAY L. LENZER

THE COYOTE IS NO HERO

He cries in the night
as we turn in our dreams.
He's no longer a trickster,
just a migrant feral canine
yelping at the stars.
How far he will go is unknown.
He sounds extremely lonely
but his clan stays together.
Some nights he ventures in
and prowls along our alleys
searching for something to eat.
He isn't joking anymore.
As time and technology grow
his life becomes more serious.
Once he was our teacher.
Now he longs to learn
how one can survive
under the moon's light
on the graded ridges
beside the new houses.

by JOHN GARMON

❋ COYOTE!

i hear him yell **coyote!** when he sees me, he chases me, sometimes he makes thunder with a shiny stick. then something whispers through leaves of Between-Others near me. he is like one of the Between-Ones, but he has no leaves, he grows different skins except on his face and hands, and he walks on his hind legs, he is not fixed in the ground like a Between-Other. the Betweens are my friends most of the time, though the little Eat-Others i feed on can also hide behind or under the Between-Others.

i don't know if **coyote!** is his cry of fear or anger, yet i have come to feel it as a part of my fur, part of my flesh, like a hit of my heartbeat. i hear **coyote!** and the sound lives in my chest. i run, but i carry that cry with me. it helps me run like a sky skin, one of those big creatures up there without eyes or heads and many times with no legs. the way they move across up there, i run dark behind Between-Others i am their color, but i cannot make thunder.

still, when sisters and brothers gather with me acrest a small hill, we sing. my chest fills with sky waking. sun is falling. sun is coming, we sing and all the wide Under enters us, all the far Up There sings in us with Under, we fill with sun sings sky down us deep.

just now i smelled one of his man-dogs,
she stank of wet that hungers me, i want
to bring her my **coyote!** run, i want to
fill her with Up There and Under, she
will have pups he will cry **coyote!** they
will lick his hands till i will laugh
and growl and sing with dark down run.

by WILL INMAN

RESETTLEMENT AT YELLOWSTONE

Wolf sits in the huge pen and waits for elk.
The gate is open. Wolf declines to run.
Once a skillful hunter from the north,
Wolf has a new home now beneath Big Sky.
Outside the pen lies roadkill oozing blood.
Wolf knows that if the gate is locked against
the handout humans call entitlement
satiety may never come again.
Big Sky turns black. The night begins to fill
with rabbits thumping fearlessly for love.
Big Sky turns gold. The day begins to fill
with herds of cream-rich buffalo, brown calves
cavorting lightly in the meadow that
provides the cud survivors of Great Fire
can ruminate contentedly upon.
Big Sky turns black. Wolf remembers moose
and mule deer and antelope and sheep.
Big Sky turns gold. Wolf's belly sounds the time
until Wolf bolts, tail high as if to flag
the dominance that followers respect.
Wolf's nose recovers pleasures of the wild.
Wolf's teeth dig deep into the keeper's gift.
Wolf's scat becomes a feisty calling card.
Home, according to Wolf, means tender game . . .
life means adaptation to the whims
of the park's most dangerous animal.

by JOANNE SELTZER

YELLOW EYES

Herodotus tells us the Athenians carved
model pillars from the jaws of *Lupus Infectus.*
—from Hobson's *Treatise on Wolves*, 1803

I.

When I first saw you
you scared me.
I would have clubbed you to death, except,
you looked at me.
And feeding you,
I saw that lemon-eyed defiance
slowly admit me into confidence.

Then the days of speaking by appearing,
so close you wore my hand as a hat.

II.

I like to wake you up with money.

One by one I place quarters on your head—
They sit there on the fur,
a strip of helmet, a metal bandage.
Don't move, now, I say
Don't move.
I pull my sheets around me,
cross myself.

Receive this money
as a banker receives ashes—
no amount will save you.

Your ears twitch,
the coins slide onto the blanket.
I count them out
and place them on your head again,
over your eyes—

Don't move, now.

III.

Tell me.

When this rag of winter
no longer binds us
will I find the lace of your bones
on the incline of a spring?

Tell me before you leave.

Let me know in that wild,
interspecies fashion
what you meant to say.

Was it the higher music of a wolfen soul
caught between feral needs and domesticity?
And if your song caught fire in me,
if we could sing in kind,
how would it go?

What would it sound like?

by PHILIP SPARACINO

❋ MOUNTAIN GOAT

Old goat gazes in drum helix,
in clear season,

lays a musty necklace down over
shoulders of his ridgeline brides.

Ruminating on the north-faced wall
he chews sorrel, grinds it down.

So, sleeping—
dreams choose him like footholds,

and waking—
hard plants
choose him like dreams.

by BILL YAKE

❋ DEER AND ROSES

All these years I've listened to complaints about deer,
the nibbles and decimation, invasion like rose rust

or powdery mildew. Nothing takes the bloom off a bush
like deer with delicate teeth, they slip everything supple

from our garden—the Iceberg roses blossom into spring,
radiant in their cold to blush bloom, and the deer take them

the way we pick pears—one white body after another.
This garden of pots and planters we came to like virgins

not knowing how deep each root must sink—the strawberry,
broad basket of leaf, gone; the *mimulus* taken down leaf

by leaf—it must be sweet. Still we talk about basil,
thick scent bending toward dinner, oregano that arrows

into the kitchen! And we take in lettuce—red-leaf,
romaine, radiccio, arugula while the deer browse.

Then at twilight, a buck, four-point and flanneled;
he tastes everything we set to soil—all the roses,

even the wild ones that arc above the window.
It isn't as if we could see him in the hazel dark—

but we can hear the snap of wilderness. So it happens—
petal by petal, he takes the roses down.

by NANCY CHERRY

❋ FOUR A.M. JOURNEY

Our accommodations at a Yosemite Institute Elderhostel were rather spartan—a nine-by-twelve-foot cabin WOB (without bath), as described in the information brochure. The three of us assigned to #15 were in the age group when a trip to the "B" might be the order of the night, so between the hours of three and four A.M. we might choose to make the journey solo, duo, or trio. I personally preferred going with a companion, since on a previous occasion I found myself wandering among thirty identical cabins, trying to locate #15.

On this particular night, I opted for companionship on the trip. With flashlights in hand, we took off in speedy flight on a short journey. As we skidded around the corner of the "B", an overturned trash can came into view—then the Kleenex embellished head of a large black bear emerged from the can. For a brief moment, it seemed we were eyeball to eyeball. Then as we stood transfixed, the bear slowly ambled away, no doubt thinking, why bother with them. They are just two women heading for the "B".

Later, friends asked us, "Didn't you scream or run back to your cabin?" We answered, "No, we had a mission to fulfill, so we just hurried on to the 'B'." We did wish we had taken our camera on that trip!

by ARLINE A. HILE

CUB

Cub nosed belly
between groans,
jumped back scared,
clear of swatting paw.
Alone
rise out of earth
all fur and snout
becoming Bear.
Shake off the leaves and twigs,
roar in the morning mist.

by JEFF KNORR

PART FIVE

SIX-LEGGERS OF THE REALLY WILD WEST

SUMMER GUESTS

Weather warms
thirsty ants trail in to kitchen sink
remind me of old disputes   ex-wife and I
me, armed with book on natural remedies
she, can of pesticide in hand.

Living alone now
I leave jar caps of water on counter top—
ants stream in through cracks and gaps.

I watch   hundreds of them
those coming, those going
a brief encounter   forelegs and antennae touch—
sharing the news.

Black rings of insects   line lid edges, drinking.
Why should I mind?
As long as I keep honey jar closed tight
they get into no mischief
and they are silent as the night.

by PAUL YOUNG

NATURAL SELECTION

you little moths
born tonight
welcome, cousins
to the flame of the world
you won't die
in our candles
and single lamp
(with the etched rose) tonight
our small fires
are screened
as you have noted
beware the gecko!
ah, cousins
I understand
you're too small
and taste bad

by TONY D'ARPINO

STREAK-WINGED RED SKIMMER

You linger on the brown tip of a summer green reed
like a flame on a candle at mass,
pointing my thoughts heavenward

above this earth
where humans seem the only species
incapable of evolving,

while Malathion threatens the midges and your kin.
You hang on,
you burn like fire in the mid-day sun,

as if purifying,
transforming man's ominous intentions.
You pose on your reedy throne

like Arthur at his round table,
insuring by your radiant presence
the dream of Camelot.

Still alive, still one ember glowing
in the midst of ashes
and the fumes of Malathion.

by DIANA WOODCOCK

CRANE FLIES

Limp with restlessness she stretches
an adolescent dangle of arms and head
across my fence. I shift on the chaise,
settle into a posture of conversation,
but she can't carry words across a wall
of crane flies stuttering between us
ghost threads raveling in the formality of light.

Not until dusk weighs upon us
like a secret does she confide:
"Watching them mate is my hobby."
She rides her giggles home
as I ease into twilight, sink back
into a silver pitch of stars.

Crane flies bounce against window screens
huddle in a convention on my glass door,
not mating that I can see—just wanting in.
Scant lives, and that is all they do, butting
against the magnitude of simple desires.

by LINDA A. VANDLAC

BOX ELDERS: JOURNEY TO A DISTANT STAR

Sitting here on a hot July day night—night of the 4th of July, as a matter of fact, by my light, notebook open, waiting. It may even be July fifth by now. The fan is running by the front door, pointing into Mark's room, Audrey is at a friend's down the street, Debbie is in bed asleep, as is Mark. I picked up an aiming telescope for our telescope we bought to go out and look at Halley's Comet, which we never did—there was a box elder bug on it. An immature box elder bug only about a quarter inch long. I looked at it for a while. They are pretty creatures with their black and red coloring, their delicate legs and antennae: they have six legs and two fairly smooth antennae that seem to be jointed about two-thirds of the way up the shaft, and seem flexible all the length. I turned the little aiming telescope around; the box elder went for a ride—up or down seemed to make no difference to it. Its mouth parts are too small for me to see, but I could see once when its eyes caught the light in just the right way, that it has pretty chocolate brown eyes about the size of fly specks. The animal seemed to be content to sit on the little red scope (it is a scope about the size of a fat pen), but I decided to get him to move a bit. I changed the angle of the scope and the animal went to the other end. It circled around the top and went back, went around, moved length- and width-wise on the tube. Coming around the top end one time it stopped to clean its front legs together, as you have seen a fly do—then it cleaned off its left antenna in the same manner. It made me think of a cat, cleaning itself so carefully. Then it continued on around on its journey up and down and around the tube. It seemed to me that it sensed its way while afoot by the use of the antennae which it moved up and down alternately. It probably receives a different reading, as a bat does by echo location from each antenna. A curious, but not unexpected, thing was that when it approached my flesh, my fingertips, it avoided. It stopped each time it neared my actual body part by just a tiny fraction of a space, but never touched. I had earlier blown lightly on its antennae to see if that would cause any great clamor, but it didn't seem to mind either the stench of my breath or the puff of air: a movement which I have seen send spiders into frenzies of activity—one which surely must represent some sort of presence to small animals of a possible threat or a possible meal; but which had no observable effect upon the adolescent box elder. Probably not being a hunter-killer (I guess), the box elder is not attuned to this sort of movement. I can only guess that it was my body warmth which turned it away from my fingertips, although it could have been my scent. However, I tend to think it is not the scent because it is living in a house filled with my scent, in my cave, so to speak, and it must have through all the years of evolution come to regard it as a scent which can be ignored, for all practical purposes. So I am guessing that the stimulus the antennae recognized was body heat, which is not to say that the antennae are not also used for smelling (or sensing pheromones). After it worked its way around on the scope for a while, and had come up to my fingertips five or six times and not been bothered, it finally ventured up into the hairy jungles of my fingers, then worked its way across the foothills and ravines of my knuckles. I made a pen bridge for it, which it took across the precipice to my right forearm, where it staggered around in the hair for a minute, then sensed the air for a while with its flexible antennae, and looked as if it were looking out across the vast spaces far off a mountaintop, over toward the marble-topped end-table from whence it had come, then stretched and flexed and steadied, and tilted its body forward as I have seen the birds do so many times, then blurred its little wings and flew, back to my table which is its home.

2

Little box elder lands on table before me. Flat black wings with white strip on outer edge. Red tip on tail. Wings have a triangle design on them when folded together, as they are at all times except in flight. Then from the triangle another pattern made of angles like you sometimes see formed in panes of ice, but perfectly symmetrical. The thorax has two large red dots on it, intended to look like eyes, perhaps. In the center of the thorax, a small triangle is base to base with the larger triangle formed by the pattern on the wings. In the triangle in between the wings there is a shape like that of a t-bone steak bone, the sharp point pointing toward the tail of the animal. I see now how the antennae are jointed in four parts. The legs are delicately proportioned, and in this instance the back ones are drawn up, because of the angle at which the animal now sits on the side of my finger—drawn up as people do when sleeping on their backs—one leg high up, the other stretched out. This little animal will sit still for ten minutes, perfectly immobile, and then suddenly scurry away almost as if it were possessed of some idea about something it remembered just now it had to do. Another thing I have seen it do is to play dead. When it first landed on the table and I tried to get it to climb up on my finger so I could look more closely at it, it became frightened and ran; seeing that I would trap it any which way it would turn, it flipped over onto its back and placed its legs over its body, in the universal pose of death. I was afraid that I had killed it accidentally while trying to pick it up, but when I placed my finger gently on top of it, it reached up and grabbed hold for the ride. Is it possible the little animal was spoofing me by playing dead—I mean spoofing not in earnest but in play? After I held it on my finger for some time, about ten minutes, and looked at it, it made its mad chase up into the hairy part of my fingers, on the backs of them, stopped a while to feel out the grass with its feelers, then charging through, onto the flat part of my palm, it said goodbye, and flew again. It flew up to the light above and crashed into the glass chimney around the bulb, flew around a few more seconds as if it couldn't quite decide, then landed on a part of the lamp and stayed—another journey to a distant star complete.

by GREG KOSMICKI

CRICKET

Below many moons,
winding itself
like a wrist-watch
tighter and tighter
without stopping
hour after hour
night after night
until one night,
walking many nights,
its mate arrives
and the mainspring breaks.

by BOO HEISEY

DUTIFUL POEM

I must kill the roach
in my jewelry box!
A mobile dark opal,
baroque pearl, tiger's eye,

does she seek glitter
for her drab life?
Attracted by powder,
my scent on pearls,

does she want Chanel #5?
And as she cracks
old glue of fittings
in her mandibles,

does she dream
of returning to oceans
as a trilobite
decked out in gold?

I should kill the roach
in my jewelry box.
I will wait at least
until next week . . .

by ELISAVIETTA RITCHIE

DIVINITY

What?
You'd like to feel good about yourself?
Okay then, listen to this—
there's a little bit of god in you.

But wait!
Don't puff up your chest just yet.
Don't fan out those tail feathers—
I'm not through!

There's a little bit of god in you—
it's true.
But there's a little bit of god
in cockroaches too.

by PAUL YOUNG

BUG

I lie in quiet night
reading   in blanket bundled comfort
when movement   at the edge of vision
draws me away from my book.
Here, another summer insect
I've never seen before.
It crawls across pillow
slow legs   swinging along like oars
halts before me   nose to nose   antennae
wavering.

I scramble from covers   to my desk
find magnifying glass   slip back onto bed
carefully hold it   inches away
a world opens—
vein laced wings
furry body, spotted in orange
black, multi-lensed eyes   I exhale
from the side of my mouth   so not to disturb
hold breath   heartbeat against mattress
till I can't contain, and gasp,
"You're so beautiful!"

She knows how I feel.

by PAUL YOUNG

A BLACK BUG

You might laugh to see the tiny black bug making its trail across the sand in front of you—wandering aimlessly, in search of who knows what? And for what reason must it run up against a brown and rotting piece of leaf or charge headlong into a hole from which it cannot even extract itself—what a pitiful existence! First you watch it run one way, then another. It is hard to tell by looking at it, from your vantage point, whether it is governed by its instincts, or its will, or by some outside force much greater than it, operating it like a remote control toy for its own pleasure. You may even come to think the little black bug was somehow placed there for your pleasure: as if there were some reason you happened to come upon this spot of sun to watch another creature, even lowlier, as you think, than yourself, struggle through the apparently absurd exigencies of its daily life—for what? Perhaps your edification or pleasure. And who watches you?

by GREG KOSMICKI

PART SIX

EIGHT-LEGGERS OF THE REALLY WILD WEST

MY DOCTOR SUGGESTS I VACUUM MY MATTRESS

MITES: Order *Acarina*, genus *Sarcoptes*, species *S. Scabiei*

Bugs, others got, I thought. Abroad.

But, Norma informs me, everyone has them.
She's Irish, notices even what's microscopic.
Says: an Englishman travelling carries a can
of anti-mite spray for the sheets of Irish hotels.
And everywhere else on this globe
ruled by insects hungry for us.

I tear the old sheets off my bed, plunge them
in the washing machine, superhot, brimming
with bleach, drag the mattress into the dubious sun.

Next I shower, scrub with loofa and pumice stone,
shampoo till my hair falls out.
Sulphur, kerosene, should rub out the bugs—

Not bugs. Six limbs just in the larval stage.

These cousins to spiders, scorpions, ticks,
have eight legs, no waist, and a face full
of grasping, piercing and sucking devices.
Body all abdomen, the better to store
blood, if they're lucky, or flakes of food,
flowers, feathers, fuzz, debris in the dust.
Each species has its own cup of tea.

I suddenly wonder: will I miss them now,
my collection of personal parasites

swept down drains? Unless, still hungry, loyal,
they burrowed in deep, hang on . . . .

When I die, will my free-living mites?
Or accompany me toward the next world—
veer off to their own heaven and hell?
Or creep quickly away in distaste, desert
the sunk ship, find someone new to feast on?

May they take a few cells with my DNA,
and avoid fastidious Englishmen.

I towel myself dry, remake the bed.

In the World Book, Volume M, *mites share the
page with three Mitchells: John of Watergate
fame, also Margaret (Gone With the Wind), and
Maria who studied sunspots, discovered a comet.
Mites are followed by Mithras, Angel of Light.*

by ELISAVIETTA RITCHIE

SPIDERS

See, in that dark basement
I learned, like potato eyes,
how to sprout. I kept to corners.
I learned scrutiny without calling
attention to myself, small,
eyelids drooping for camouflage.
I learned how Persephone
must have felt, and roots.
They must always go down.
They must feel out opposition:
rocks, building foundations, pipes.

It was hard, then, adjusting
to air without mold. Hard to hear
above all that honking and talk.
Hard to see the good out of which
I came. Now I live above ground, two
or more stories up if I can. I lay me
down in the dark with night lights,
knowing some morning I won't wake.
Meanwhile, the spiders
remind me: I let them have
the run of my house.

by SUSAN LANDGRAF

ARCTOSA

(Burrowing Wolf Spider)

i've seen you, little princess
raise your blackberry tiara, then
go winking down your hole

i've waited for you breathlessly
a magician emerging from her own hat
slowly, one tarsus on the turret
then leg up to the femur
second pair, carapace
woolly fangs, periscope eyes
that timid mesmer's expression
in the center of your face
as deep and dark as your hole

i've seen you burrowing, she-wolf
excavating fangfuls of sand
pushing loads the size of your gut
up the sides of your pit
and pitch them with cyclopean might
a whole hole's length

i've seen you in your suburbs
domestic goddess and your sisters
sunning your arms and face
false heather your hedgerow
beach grass your sweeping palm
you wait for the neighbors to walk by
and snatch them down for lunch
unless they have enormous feet
then all arms go up in shriek
as you surrender to the hole

i've seen you with that man
femme fatale out of the fifties
you'll take him down to explore
every shaft and cavity
carelessly tossing the spent corpse
outside your hole sweet hole

i've seen you sunning your eggsac
a diamond studded pillow
turning it on warm sand
dreaming of your brood
wondering when they'll get on your back
but you give it hollow abandon
at a predator's approach

i've seen you leave the circle
to catch a flying feast
and then i covered your sipapu
only to witness your anxious breakdown
shock, xenophobic withdrawal, no retreat

i know
for hole is where the heart is
your wishing well of safety
with its secret passages
you slip into in case of
flood or flicker's tongue
wasp or sand castle sweep

i see all and nothing
enchantress of the dark circle
who i return to at every opportunity
to see how the lady vanishes

i wonder where you go
in winter, persephone
as you stare toward me
with those pomegranate eyes
i patiently wait for you to fully emerge
tentative as early spring

by MATT WELTER

SHADOW OF A CLOUD

creeping along
the cool New Mexico desert.
Crawling up and down arroyos
yet never shading the tops
of mesquite or soap yucca stalks.
Look up.
Not a cloud in the sky.

For this is not a shadow
it is the tarantula migration
and that is why the road is closed,
as we quietly wait outside our cars,
behind the barrier and conservation guards.
Some of us look on with binoculars
all of us feel like heat waves:
quiet, our spirits evaporating.

The biker that reported them still stands there
dark, grizzled, scorched
like a bug-eyed sentinel.
He says he could have smashed them
by the hundreds,
but he stopped in disbelief,
watched them all jumping one direction.
Then he wheeled back around.

A tourist breaks our silence,
sticks his head out of his rental car
shouts, "Come on! I got somewhere to go!"
Our spirits cringe like tarantulas.
We think back at him,
"So do they."

by MATT WELTER

ALIEN

We are not alone and never have been.

Having travelled this gauzy firmament
suspended through space deep winter
the mothership idles, her cotton craft
going almost, almost undetected.

Tissued to our curtain
now rawly exposed
this Venetian Red spider
this lunar umbrella
folded and dry
robot-jointed
with one bamboo needle begins creakily to probe.

Signing hopefully, the traveller's mudra
she comes following maps given light years ago—

Ringing the Milky Way she has birthed and become
swirl and cluster wriggling points of light
pinpoint beings her myriad children
an army of abdomens, nesting flexing
little legs saluting the sun of May.

Concerned to meet their teeming force
we take them to the porch and let them go
gently, gently on the warming winds of earth
final destination yet unknown.

Bold starseed babies, Red Rusty Mother
flying now through weird receptive skies—

Think of them, will you, when humans speak of Roswell
when they reach with longing for big-headed mystery
for cheap metallic craft lying broken in the desert.

by PATRICIA CATTO

WOVEN SYMBIOSIS

My feet crunch in black lodgepole ash
as I walk among the charred totems.

I find a tiny orb weaver spider in her web.
This place seemed lifeless until now.

I bend down to get a closer look.
Gnats begin to bite my cheeks.

Gently, I brush them from my face,
easing them into her thin dinner plate.

She dives down to wrap and drink
each rare and struggling morsel.

Her fill is three.
Theirs is never enough.

Mine is when she helps
the sixth wriggle free.

by MATT WELTER

PART SEVEN

EVEN-MORE-LEGGERS OF THE REALLY WILD WEST

BORN AGAIN

Soft and plump
I crawl on milkweed's
pale sour stalks
nibbling leaves
my emptiness unappeased
by the bitter
lacemaking

Soon I will spin
a silken stalk
and dissolve inside my sack
of a skin
forget
the jeers of birds
my own green
and vulnerable
body

Next time I'll try
black threads for legs
flowerscope eyes
a tongue coiled deep
in my throat
and wings
of powder and silk
uncrumpled
into tapestries

A breath body
drifting and tilting
through bright blue summer
and south to Mexico
no keel
no heft
tattered as a leaf ravaged
by caterpillars
longing for a home
for heaviness

by ANN WEILER WALKA

ATTRIBUTES OF THE CONTRIBUTORS

PAYING TRIBUTE TO LEAST LOVED BEASTS OF THE REALLY WILD WEST

CONTRIBUTORS

RUTH ADAMS has lived and gardened on the outskirts of "Greater Los Angeles" for almost fifty years and has always enjoyed the small creatures with whom she shares the garden. She writes that a surprising variety of wild things actually thrive in and around this big city. "We have raccoons that run races on our roof, possums that grub up worms in our seed beds. Skunks abound and foxes reside in our neighboring hills." She says these are in addition to the birds and butterflies she tries to encourage in her plantings. "What a dreary place the world would be without them!"

ALAN STUART AUSTIN was born in Lincoln in the United Kingdom and has traveled the world marveling at the diversity of creation, whether it be watching Christmas Island frigate birds or the few remaining pythons in Singapore cruising past his doorstep. He currently teaches Senior English at Xavier College Prep and takes long walks in a fascinating landscape quickly being eaten up by urban sprawl.

SAM BARASCH wrote his untitled poem in fall of 1995, several months after seeing a bald eagle for the first time. He was on a weekend canoe trip, and while canoeing down the Wisconsin River, he and his friends saw the eagle hunting for fish. "Seeing the magnificent power of an animal that was nearly brought to extinction really moved me, and I have tried to capture that sense of awe in my poem." He writes that he "earns bread with programming," and that he has significant interests in poetry on the Internet.

JEN BLACKHORSE, who informs about heritage of a mother who was Sioux Indian and a father who was Danish "with a little Irish and Japanese," currently lives in Marshall, Minnesota, with a dog whose name is Maya.

NORAH BOOTH grew up wild in the Sonoran Desert, friends with turtles, tarantulas, toads, lizards, scorpions, snakes and other critters and varmints. "We destroy the habitat of these creatures, and we will be sorry. We could live with them, if we had the imagination." She writes and performs, travels, and teaches writing.

JANINE CANAN is a poet, psychiatrist, founder of Port Townsend's Center for Integration, devoted member of the Worldwide Women's Party, and author of *Her Magnificent Body: New & Selected Poems* and *She Rises like the Sun: Invocations of the Goddess by Contemporary American Women Poets.* A native Californian, she now lives in Port Townsend, Washington, with her Samoyed dog, her Siamese cat, the countless birds that nest around her house, as well as "the guardian cedars and firs, the talkative waters of the Juan de Fuca Strait, the stones whose fabulous stories strew the sand, and, overhead, the ever-changing, light-bringing sky." A new collection of her poetry, *Changing Woman*, is soon to be published.

EIDO FRANCES CARNEY is a Soto Zen priest/teacher at Olympia Zen Center in Washington. She also teaches writing and humanities at South Puget Sound Community College. She is a graduate of the writing program at San Francisco State University. "All over the world, humble creatures are reminding us to listen to the primal sanity of what is natural and whole. The call of a loon at dawn, wing flap of crow in fog, opossum hissing in moonlight, cat mewing in the alley, squirrels chasing along telephone wires—these brethren are our powerful and abiding teachers."

PATRICIA CATTO, Associate Professor of Literature at the Kansas City Art Institute, writes and lectures on the sacred interconnectedness of all life. Through poetry she seeks to reclaim a language of worship, a way of praising that which goes unnoticed, unloved, unseen. Of unloved creatures she says, "More like gods than demons, they must be honored for themselves, not made to carry the brutish shadows of human beings." In 1991, she published *Wife of Geronimo's Virile Old Age: 17 Poems from Cochise County*, a chronicle of her relationship with the Sonoran Desert.

NANCY CHERRY writes, "A year in Inverness where the fox lived, where the bobcat prowled the dusk, where the stars were the only light on moonless nights. Raccoons haunted the garbage bins, skunks inhabited the basement, true owners. Field mice, the voles often met their fates at the foot of the stairs where the cat sat. Varied thrush and scrub jay clung to telephone wires, flew through the tangle of blackberry, tanoak, then away. Crows made themselves heard at all hours and the osprey cried and dove into Tomales Bay, catching bass and flying the streaming fish to the nests, huge woven basketry caught in the snags of oak and eucalyptus. Every season, a new hatching, the egg-white heads of newborns barely cresting the edge of the nest, fed on fish high over our heads." She currently lives in Fairfax where "a pair of red-tail hawks sail above the woods," and where she raises zucchini, eggplant, tomatoes, and cucumbers in the deep end of a filled-in swimming pool. She is the editor of *Fish Dance: A Poetry Calendar & Newsletter for the North Bay*. Her work has appeared in various journals including *Poetry Flash, Green Fuse, Palo Alto Review*, and *Lucid Stone*.

BILL COWEE writes that he was raised in Montana by good parents not blessed with riches so native animals were his family's food. "After a menu of venison, elk, duck, pheasant and trout, beef or chicken was a treat. But I learned wonder and respect for wilderness, endless cascade of beaver dam, red picture writing mysterious on granite, the way campfires seem to melt stories out of people." He says that he likes to be the keen observer, elbow in the ribs saying, "Did you see that?" He describes himself as an accountant, founding member of the Ash Canyon Poets in Carson City, Nevada, and a "simple earwig rancher noted for my recipe of Chuckwagon Earwig Stew." His poetry has appeared in numerous publications, including *Interim, Green Fuse, Journal of Southwest Literature, Northwest Literary Forum, South Dakota Review, Sonoma Mandala, Concho River Review*, and *Desert Wood*, an anthology of Nevada poets published by the University of Nevada Press.

TONY D'ARPINO has lived with the bugs of glory, giant spiders, and assorted flyers in Idaho, California, Oregon, and Hawaii. Recent poetry has appeared in *The Bloomsbury Review, Chaminade Literary Review*, and *Nebo*. Books include *The Tree Worshipper* and *The Shape of the Stone*.

GRACE DEER has spent most of her life living with the hills and mountains of central Arizona. She has sought the places (within and without) where she could touch the earth. "My animal-relations have been gentle and awesome both in our encounters. Sometimes they talk. Like the time the coyote and I were under cover within the same oak elder, in the midst of the killing fields; it was deer-hunting season, and we were both feeling hunted. He showed me how to become invisible to those looking for prey. Like the javelina, he told me his truth." She was awarded a 1997 Creative Writing Fellowship by the Arizona Commission on the Arts.

SUNNIE EMPIE, who lives in north Scottsdale, Arizona, is a freelance writer and author of environmental articles. She writes that the evening our letter of acceptance arrived, Diamondback showed up to claim congratulatory remarks. "She had given me a poem, and now, a brief story of my relationship with Earth's creatures. I lit three luminarias, each only two feet apart, while Diamondback remained quietly curled up in the dark beside the middle one! We've shared this landscape for years. The living desert where roadrunner tries to eat snake who is ingesting rabbit; where Diamondbacks dance and mate on sun-warmed boulders."

CYNTHIA GALLAHER is the author of two published books of poetry, *Night Ribbons* and *Private, On Purpose*, and is contributing editor and poetry columnist for *Chicago Books in Review*. *Night Ribbons* was honored by the Illinois Library Association and the Chicago Public Library. Her poem "Armadillo" is part of a newly completed full poetry manuscript entitled *Earth Elegance*. Other poems from the manuscript have appeared in *Gaia*, *Green Fuse*, *Sing Heavenly Muse*, *EarthTones* anthology (Gypsy/Vergin Press) and *Environment: Essence and Issue* (Pig Iron Press), among others. She has served in the Shorekeepers program of the Lake Michigan Federation and is a former board member of Illinois Consumers for Safe Food.

JOHN GARMON writes that his poetry, which has appeared in the *Southern Poetry Review*, *Ploughshares*, *New Mexico Humanities Review*, *Prairie Schooner*, and other journals, was shaped by rural experiences offered by growing up in a small farming and ranching town in the Texas panhandle. His early memories are of listening to coyotes howling at the edge of town and, during the day, watching "chicken hawks" circling above his parents' tiny edge-of-the-town farm. His major memory of a brush with the natural world was a run-in with a bobcat; it was running away from his brothers, who were at one end of a small canyon, when he was going to meet them—the bobcat was caught between. It quickly climbed to the top of the ravine and wasn't seen again; but, for a moment, he looked into the eyes of a wild creature and recognized its fear, and wondered if it saw the same in his eyes. Another close call was when he was a young Marine in Guam in the late fifties; he was swimming in the Pacific when he was hit by what he thought was a shark. His companions on the beach said it was probably just a dolphin, but he kept dreaming for a few nights afterwards that it could indeed have been a shark. John and his wife, Pat, currently live in Kansas City, Kansas.

M. CORBIN GOULD loves the southwest desert and all its creatures, but she feels a special kinship with snakes.

BOO HEISEY expresses, "As a youngster on my way home from school one rainy day, my relationship with nature began when I encountered a muster of snails forced from cover by the rain. My mother wasn't pleased when she opened the lunch box I had left on the kitchen counter to find it completely filled with the live escargot. From her reaction that day, I learned to respect wildlife from a distance and leave it in its place. As a freelance writer, I have time to reflect on the nature of things—including nature, believing we should live off nature's interest, not her principal."

ARLINE A. HILE writes that the outdoors, with all its wonders, has always been important to her. One summer she spent a month in Kenya on a camping safari. "Each day was spent animal viewing inside one of the Parks. At night animal calls and cries were wonderful to hear. A balloon ride high over hundreds of animals, while hiking, a close encounter with a Cape Buffalo, watching a baboon remove the contents of a tent, and riding a camel were some of the highlights of the safari." She also lived for twelve years in a remote area in the Blue Ridge Mountains, where deer and raccoon were often her visitors and, when the ground was snow covered, wild turkeys would come close to the house scratching for food. "This location, with its star-studded skies and crystal clear air, made it a wonderful place to live."

RITA A. HOEFLEIN describes herself as a die-hard hiker who has acquired a great deal of respect for the desert and its inhabitants. "On more than one occasion, I have seen people kill snakes out of fear or for sport. These experiences have always left me with an inexplicable sense of loss, and I am grateful for the opportunity to say something on their behalf. If a vote were taken today that included all the members of the food chain, I think we would win—hands down—the title, *Least Loved Beast of the Really Wild West.*"

MARY WILLETTE HUGHES writes that she is sixty-four, a wife, mother of seven and grandmother to fourteen children. She grew up on a farm in southern Minnesota. "It was there that I first learned to appreciate the diversity of animal life as an integral and necessary part of farm existence. The older I grew, the more I marveled at birds, animals and fish . . . each unique and beautiful in their own way. In 1989, after our children were on their own, I discovered the world of writing poetry—a new dimension and zest in my life. I am learning how to speak/sing in this new voice."

THOMAS HULEN, "Thom" to friends and family, has been exploring the southwest most of his 41 years on the planet. As Curator of Education and Park Naturalist at Pueblo Grande Museum and Cultural Park, he spends a considerable amount of time learning about and sharing his knowledge of the cultural and natural history of the Sonoran Desert and associated biomes. He is happily married to a wonderful woman and is the very proud father of a beautiful and bright daughter.

WILL INMAN was born in North Carolina in 1923, and his work has appeared in hundreds of publications and anthologies. He writes that his major public appearance took place before the House Committee on UnAmerican Activities in 1956. He also writes that it took a long time for him to realize that each human psyche is an ark of all living creatures and that the only real way to "catch" or "possess" them is to nurture them in the wild, thus spiritually keeping some of our real selves untamed and free. He is retired, still busy writing and leading a weekly writing workshop in Tucson.

JEFFREY JOHNSON was born and raised in a small town in rural Minnesota. "As a boy I spent many happy hours at the river and in the ditches and fields around my home, picking up evidence of yesterday's stories and clues to the mysteries I made up for myself."

MICHAEL KIRILUK writes, "I grew up an isolated child, alone, daily, in a world of field and sky. My only companions, my first teachers, jack rabbits, vultures, scrub jays. Their lessons have continued as my pool of teachers has grown to include the philosophers, bandits and statesmen of mountain and desert. My membership in the community of Ash Canyon Poets in Carson City, Nevada, presents me with a unique environment where I may study and explore the knowledge that I have gained from creatures some see as less than worthy of reflection."

JEFF KNORR lives in Portland, Oregon, and teaches English at Clackamas Community College. Aside from his chapbook, *Up We Travelled*, his work has appeared in a number of journals including *Reed Magazine*, *Suisun Valley Review*, and *Fireweed* and is forthcoming in anthologies by Adrienne Lee Press and Black Buzzard Press. He is currently editor of the new *Clackamas Literary Review*.

GREG KOSMICKI expresses that he has loved to watch bugs and other living things since he was a little boy. Some of his favorite and most memorable things to read have been writings about nature in one form or another: *Keith County Journal* by John Janovy; *The Insect World of J. Henri Fabre*, edited by Edwin Way Teale; *Pilgrim at Tinker Creek* by Annie Dillard, the poems, novels, and essays of Wendell Berry, and Carl Sagan's *Cosmos*. He writes that he "had an unfortunate few years of killing pheasants and ducks to do the macho thing," but that he "grew out of that into a vegetarian, over the gentling years."

SUSAN LANDGRAF is a photographer and writer whose poems have appeared in *Ploughshares*, *Nimrod*, *Calyx*, *Spoon River Quarterly*, *Small Pond Literary Magazine*, and other literary journals. She has won Pablo Neruda, Stafford, Grayston, and Academy of Poets awards. In addition, she was awarded first place in a poetry competition sponsored by the Society for Humanistic Anthropology/American Anthropological Association. Susan writes, "We share this world—with each other, the beasts, the trees, the moon, the cliff sides and rivers. The butterfly flapping its wings in France affects the wind velocity in Massachusetts; to me that means we must take time to really see our world and understand the parts we play. Such diversity; yet, at the same time, I have seen patterns and been awed at the order within the diversity. How amazing it all is—millipedes, dragonflies, bloodsuckers, bats, wolves, quarks, stars, huckleberries, moss, sandstone, and spiders."

MELANIE LEFEVER credits her grandmother with passing on to her grandchildren an interest in natural history. "Farm-raised Grandma devised outings to bird sanctuaries, created a backyard garden with us (her sterile apartment building had no green space), and introduced us to liverworts, squirrels, salamanders, and slugs. My 'home' was a college-campus arboretum, where I played under a *Franklinia* tree, a species no longer found anywhere in the wild. Later, I studied and worked in green houses for seventeen years. My desire to write comes from a love of languages (classical and modern) and a need to extract meaning from simple things. Observation of creatures in nature is revelatory. We learn anew each time, and creative endeavor only begins to sustain these perceptions, recapturing them in reflection for others to share. I believe that any hint of wisdom, understanding, and perhaps even change, is possible only after an acceptance of people and things as they are."

URSULA K. LE GUIN, author of *Buffalo Gals and Other Animal Presences*, is a widely known American writer whose works include science fiction, fantasy, young adult fiction, children's books, essays, and poems. Her recent books include *Four Ways to Forgiveness* (HarperCollins); *The Twins, the Dream: Poetry by Ursula K. Le Guin and Diana Bellessi* (Arte Publico Press); and a new translation of the *Tao Te Ching*, forthcoming from Shambhala Publications. Among her best known novels are *The Left Hand of Darkness*, *The Dispossessed*, *Always Coming Home*, and the Earthsea Cycle: *A Wizard of Earthsea*, *The Tombs of Atuan*, *The Farthest Shore*, and *Tehanu*. She has received numerous awards including the Nebula, Hugo, Kafka, World Fantasy, and National Book Awards.

MAY L. LENZER has always been enchanted by animals and nature. "At seven I discovered horses, deciding I would become a veterinarian. Never achieving that, I have been an animal rights/environmental activist, wildlife rehabilitator, and involved in the placement of unwanted domestic animals. Married, with a son, we live in panhandle Florida with a houseful of rescued dogs and cats, birds, donkeys, a quarter horse, and anything wild that needs care. I enjoy butterfly gardening, photography, and writing about the incredible things I continue to observe in our shrinking natural world."

EDWARD C. LYNSKEY writes that his poetry, which frequently uses wildlife and animal rights themes, has appeared in *The Atlantic Monthly, American Poetry Review, Commonweal, Poetry Northwest*, and *Chicago Review*. His poem, "Cry of the Night Heron," is due to appear in *The Great Blue Heron and Other Poems Anthology* (Adrienne Lee Press). He has also reviewed many animal rights and nature texts for the *San Francisco Chronicle, East West Journal, Columbus-Dispatch, Arizona Quarterly*, and *North Dakota Quarterly*. "Having been raised in rural Virginia, as well as having hiked in New Mexico's Sangre de Cristo Mountains, I've grown to appreciate wild critters, even the less than glamorous ones."

JO NELSON has been a poet in residence for the Washington State Arts Commission and has taught French, German, and English in Maryland and Colorado. She now writes, teaches poetry seminars, and is rehabilitating a house and small farm. Her poetry has been published in numerous national magazines and anthologies. Nature is the source of much of her writing. Her poem "Rattles" was inspired by an actual place in southwestern Colorado where rattlesnakes are the guardians of an old cemetery as well as some outstanding petroglyphs.

JIM NOLLMAN plays music with wild animals. Over the past twenty-five years he has performed on oceans, plains and jungles around the world, producing musical events that permit him to interact with creatures both wet and dry, big and little, including frogs, turkeys, buffalo, monkeys, and whales. His books include *Dolphin Dreamtime* (Bantam) and *Why We Garden* (Henry Holt). His audio cassettes include

Orcas Greatest Hits (Interspecies) and *Playing Music with Animals* (Smithsonian).

PAMELA J. PADGETT resides in Seattle, Washington, where she works part-time at a local bookstore while completing the University of Washington's Certificate Writing Program. Poetry calls up her biology major, several years experience in the Alaska seafood industry, and affection for the uncommonly common things. Her work has been published in *Slightly West*, and will appear in the next issues of *Sunstone* and *Yet Another Small Publication.*

BINNIE PASQUIER writes that her years in Northern California still figure powerfully in her poetry. Her poem "Encounter" is the direct result of a dream following a day's swimming and climbing over boulders in a foothills creek. Upon first seeing the cougar crouched on the rock next to her, she was afraid, but the fear left as she listened to the water and examined the beauty of the creature close to her. Now living in the heavily developed East, she still looks for sea lions and listens for the rattle of snakes though she knows they can only live with her there in dreams.

G. L. PETTIGREW received his B.A. in Biology from Earlham College in 1995, and he will soon begin graduate studies in zoology. He has an inordinate fondness for lizards.

KENNETH POBO teaches English at Widener University. His most recent poetry collection is *A Barbaric Yawp on the Rocks* (Alpha Beat Press). Of beasts he says, "I like all the beasts, the stranger the better. Snakes got a bum rap in *Genesis.* They're actually beautiful—and if one did talk, it would tell us to respect it and not be so uppity. Rats serve us well as metaphors—i.e., 'you dirty rat.' Actually, people are dirtier than rats, so it's a case of misplaced anger." He collects, as a hobby, '60s records, especially those by Tommy James, Tommy Roe, April Stevens, and others.

MATT RASMUSSEN was raised in the Midwest but moved to an island in Puget Sound in 1979, when he was 13. He has spent many days and nights since then ensconced in the Cascade Mountains of Washington and Oregon, watching, listening, and learning from the creatures that live there. He holds a journalism degree from Columbia University in New York City, and worked for five years at newspapers. He now lives in Oregon's Willamette Valley, where he earns his keep as a freelance writer and editor of an environmental journal.

BEATRICE RICHMOND, that long-ago major in zoology at Mills College (Class of '46), shaped a lifetime of respect for the natural world. A retired elementary teacher, she describes herself as "a right-brain, creative person" who is apt to do the unusual. "I live in a wild and natural part of the world—rural Arizona—and am often out rambling alone. On 'their turf' I am the interloper; it is up to me to respect their habits, their behavior, their environment. On 'my turf' I sometimes have to remove or destroy such things as spiders, feeling the need to be pardoned (by them) for this action." She lived and taught for many years on the Navajo Reservation and learned at least as much from the Navajo and the Hopi as they learned from her. She writes, "Ecology? They invented it!"

ELISAVIETTA RITCHIE, whose work has appeared in *Poetry, American Scholar, New York Times, Christian Science Monitor, Washington Post,* numerous anthologies, and other publications in the U.S. and abroad, edited *The Dolphin's Arc: Poems on Endangered Creatures of the Sea.* Her poetry collections include *The Arc of the Storm, Elegy for the Other Woman, Tightening the Circle Over Eel Country* (which won the Great Lakes Colleges Association's 1975-76 New Writer's Award), *Raking the Snow* (which won the Washington Writer's Publishing House 1981-82 competition), and *Wild Garlic: The Journal of Maria X.* Four of the stories in her collection, *Flying Time,* were PEN Syndicated Fiction winners. Elements of the animal, vegetable, and mineral kingdoms permeate her work. As an occasional poet-in-the-schools, she encourages students and teachers to focus on the natural world and environmental concerns. "I just get people (adults and children) to write about twigs and bugs and lost creatures (from the creature's viewpoint) or whatever comes."

KATE ROBINSON is a native of the Midwest who has had a "twenty-five year love affair with Arizona in her many guises and lived in six of her fourteen counties." Currently she resides in Chino Valley, Arizona, with the youngest pair of her four children. "Besides javelina, I count among my friends a Gila monster, skunks, most horned lizards, various snakes, ravens, a tarantula or two, and stink beetles. They graciously overlook my aspirations as poet, songwriter, and student of anthropology, and they allow me to be just another manifestation of Spirit, as they are."

MEREDITH SABINI has a blended career as an essayist and poet, dream researcher and clinical psychologist. Dreams provide the basis for her creative and professional writing. She taught writing courses, dream seminars, and Jungian psychology at the California School of Professional Psychology in 1980-86 and has been an editor at *Psychological Perspectives* (published by the C. G. Jung Institute of L.A.) since 1980. She attended Squaw Valley Writers' Conference in 1990 and Napa Valley Poetry Workshop in 1991. Her publications include personal essays, cultural commentaries, dream research articles, film and book reviews, editorials on eco-psychology, and studies of shamanism and visionary religious experiences. Her work has appeared in *ArtScan, Mycena, Pearl, Gaia, Mediphors, Hot Flash, Writing on the Edge, Transformation, Resurgence* (London), *Chrysalis* (Swedenborg Fdtn.), *Journal of Women & Religion, Anima, Quadrant, Elmwood Quarterly, Dream Networker, Journal of Analytical Psychology, Psychological Perspectives,* and other publications. She is native to Berkeley and of Amish ancestry.

PAUL SCHULLERY, a historian by training and a naturalist by avocation, is the author, co-author, or editor of more than 20 books about nature, conservation, and outdoor sport, including *Mountain Time: A Yellowstone Memoir, American Fly Fishing: A History,* and *The Bears of Yellowstone.* He has written for many popular and technical periodicals, including *BioScience, The New York Times, Encyclopedia Britannica Yearbook of Science and the Future,* and *Field & Stream.* He is an affiliate professor of history at Montana State University and an adjunct professor of American Studies at the University of Wyoming.

JOANNE SELTZER shares her home in upstate New York with her husband, a cat, and occasional drop-in field mice. She attributes her love of nature to her childhood in Detroit, which made visits to an aunt in Michigan's Upper Peninsula seem like mythic journeys to paradise. She has published hundreds of poems in literary journals. Her suite of poems entitled "A Place for Mother" is included in the award-winning anthology *When I Am an Old Woman I Shall Wear Purple*, and she has published three chapbooks: *Adirondack Lake Poems*, *Suburban Landscape*, and *Inside Invisible Walls*.

WILLIAM SHELDON lives with his wife and son in Hutchinson, Kansas, where he teaches at the local community college and writes. He has spent his life in the West—in California, Colorado, Montana, and Kansas. He writes, "Consequently, it took a while before I began to understand the land and its creatures in ways beyond their 'usefulness' and began to, if I may borrow a passage from Steven Hind (who has written the best poetry about our state), 'dream a life/and a death/ in this grass.' "

GAYLE SLIVA, who lives in Gardnerville, Nevada, is a writer and mother of two children. She chose rural living over the city life when she moved from the Los Angeles area to Nevada in 1988. As an adult, she creates a wide berth between herself and the creatures that inhabit her area in hopes of letting them exist with as little disturbance from humans as possible. She is a member of the Ash Canyon Poets, and her work has been published in many literary journals including *Interim*, the *West Wind Review*, and the *Liberty Hill Poetry Review*. She is co-editor of a forthcoming anthology containing the works of the Ash Canyon Poets.

LAURA SNYDER is a lifelong naturalist whose "heart home" is in Little Fort, British Columbia, Canada. She writes that this "is the place where as a teen I sat in the boat to wait for twilight and the bats." Laura of the Woods, as she refers to herself, has gathered the fruits of 42 years of observations of her beloved woodlands into a collection of botanical and biological sketches now to be used by the University of British Columbia. "Since I was a teen, my dream was to catalog all flora and fauna of these 80 acres and the local area." Recently she has started making medicine out of local plants. She has also begun to make tinctures, oils, ointments, and cough syrups. This act, she expresses "completes the circle of my tie to this land."

PHILIP SPARACINO works as a drama therapist at a continuing day treatment center in Huntington and as a Poet-in-the-Schools for the Cold Spring Harbor School District, both of which are on Long Island, New York. He frequently uses animal imagery in his drama and writing workshops to access his clients' and students' imaginations. His poetry will be appearing in upcoming issues of *The New York Quarterly, Interim, Atom Mind*, and *Pudding Magazine*.

LAUREL SPEER, whose latest publication is a prose pamphlet titled *Blood & Puppets*, is a contributing editor for the *Small Press Review*. Having lived in Tucson, Arizona, for 25 years and having observed all manner of native wildlife in her hikes up into the hills, she has developed both a respect and love for the animals and plants whose claim to the land is first and foremost.

SUSAN TERRIS lives in San Francisco. Her recent works include *Author! Author!* and *Nell's Quilt* (Farrar, Straus & Giroux) and *Killing in the Comfort Zone* (Pudding House Press) and many journal publications including *The Antioch Review, Poet Lore, Calyx, The Midwest Quarterly, Poetry Northwest, The Spoon River Poetry Review, Southern California Anthology*, and *The Southern Poetry Review*. She is currently completing a poetry collection entitled *Wedges of Parallel Time*. She is an avid hiker of western trails, and she was leading a Harvest Moon hike when she encountered the fox about whom her poem is written.

RUSS TRAUNSTEIN, a Boston V.A. Clinical Social Worker with specialties in Substance Abuse and Post-traumatic Stress, retired in 1990. After some early successes with short stories and poetry upon his return from Europe after WWII, he just recommenced writing poetry a few years ago and has been taking workshops and classes on a regular basis. Over one hundred pieces of his have been published in roughly forty journals and magazines. He creates some short stories and sketches also, both light and serious, as with his poetry. His work has appeared in the *South Coast Poetry Journal*, the *Kentucky Poetry Journal, Psychopoetica* (U. of Hull, Hull, England), *Cadence: the Review of Jazz and Blues, Light: The Quarterly of Humorous Verse, San Fernando Poetry Journal, Puckerbrush Review, Writer's Digest*, and other publications. He recently received the first Annual Discovery

Award from the New Hampshire Council on the Arts. He also received First Prize in the Writer's Digest Annual Competition for Rhyming Verse for 1996.

LINDA A. VANDLAC currently writes in a small community north of Seattle where she teaches college part-time and sometimes works as a communication consultant. Her poems have been published in several anthologies and college/small press publications, including *The Bellingham Review* and *Permafrost*. "In my poetry, I explore topics of self-reflection that celebrate the settings, concerns, and sometimes overlooked creatures of rural life."

ANN WEILER WALKA writes, "As a poet and naturalist, I explore Home Country, both the tangible, familiar landscapes that shape and color my life and the landscapes of my imagination. In my wanderings I am struck again and again by the connections and commonalities among species, by the kinfolk I encounter in the outback." In the outdoor season, she works as a free-lance naturalist and guide for field institutes and museums. She teaches writing now and again in the winter months, in school classrooms and in informal workshops. Her poems have been printed in literary and environmental journals, and her first book, *Waterlines: Journeys on a Desert River*, was published in 1993. A Fellowship in Creative Writing, awarded by the Arizona Commission in the same year, has supported her work on a new collection of poems, *The Unknown River*. In 1994 she authored the spring edition of *Plateau: The Magazine of the Museum of Northern Arizona*, entitled "Lake Powell: A Canyon Transformed." Recently, she contributed the lead essay to *Testimony*, a book compiled by Terry Tempest Williams and Steve Trimble.

MATT WELTER grew up in eastern Washington State. He has inhabited southern New Mexico, Yellowstone, the Grand Canyon, and Death Valley. "In these and all places I love the things that people fear, despise, or are repulsed by. I love spiders, bats, and mushrooms." He has been published in many literary magazines from *Rosebud* to *Prunella Vulgaris*. Two of his books, *S.A.D. Cure* (Mother Superior Press) and *Yellowstone 88* (Hodge Podge Press), were recently published. He is currently working on an M.S. degree in Environmental Education.

THOMAS WHITEHEAD lives, works, and grows a garden in Carson City, Nevada. He protects a colony of black widow spiders in his garage and has long allowed less alienated creatures wide latitude in moving about his home and person. He writes that he feeds birds and, by extension, cats. He also expresses that most of his time spent outside his writing projects, which usually take up a part of every day, is "occupied in assiduously cultivating an appearance of abject failure in all areas of human endeavor while designing the city of crystal and gold and building prototype vehicles for a culture of poverty, voluntary or otherwise." His poetry has appeared in a variety of publications.

A. D. WINANS, whose work has appeared in many journals over the years, writes, "It angers me when I hear the media describe a killer as an 'animal.' Animals don't kill for greed or the sake of violence like humans do. Animals kill for food and survival. So when I heard that a posse was tracking down a 'vicious' mountain lion who had killed a hiker trespassing in the mountain lion's domain, it angered me. It's a known fact that a mountain lion will try at all costs to avoid contact with humans. Humans, on the other hand, think nothing of invading the animal's terrain, and when occasionally attacked (extremely rare), put out a bounty on one of nature's truly magnificent creatures."

DIANA WOODCOCK expresses that, having lived in Tibet, Macau, and Thailand, she writes poetry to promote worldwide justice and to encourage caretaking of the earth. Living among the Tibetans, where she taught English and witnessed the abuse and destruction of their fragile ecosystem and wildlife, inspired her to work as a writer to save endangered species. Her poems celebrate life even as they protest crimes against humankind and nature. She writes that she aspires to being a world citizen, a sojourner, a contemplative, and an activist—and uses her poetry to bind her to all facets of nature and humankind.

BILL YAKE, author of *Givin' Critters Short Shrift* (Radiolarian Press), for years lived in an old farm house outside of Tenino, Washington, near Scatter Creek. "Deer mice, and occasional bats, lived there as well. The mice gnawed the bar soap, leaving grooved incisor marks. A bat napping upside-down on the bathroom wall would set the cat to quivering. One spring swifts nested in the chimney. They made a racket and flew in at dusk. During summers, garter snakes and alligator lizards gathered for warmth under the black plastic spread over compost piles and hunted diligently for garden slugs." Recently he moved twenty miles north to a place on Green Cove Creek. He reports "Although the housekeeping is more rigorous now, raccoons still leave their tracks in the rare snow and quarrel in the shrubbery."

PAUL YOUNG writes that he has gravitated toward the outdoors his whole life, but when he moved to southeastern Arizona four years ago, "the quality of my intercourse with the natural world somehow broadened. A recognition dawned—the fellow creatures with whom I share this planet are as sentient and probably, given their ability to dwell here in balance, more intelligent than we humans. This awareness is reflected in my poem, 'Bug.' I am fully convinced that she is keenly cognizant not only of my presence, but of my love and appreciation for her. I am awestruck by the form to which she has evolved, and I find endless wonder in conjecturing—how does she perceive me, and this world around her?"

ADRIENNE ZAMORE, graced by their loving union, came into this world courtesy of Betty Gloria Harris and Bernhard Zamore, whose ancestors two generations back had dwelled in Austria, Russia, Poland, and England. Through ancestral bloodlines she was blessed with an inherent fondness and empathy for creatures nonhuman. This trait manifested so dominantly within her that she was particularly receptive, at the age of two, to the scrub jay who often flew down and perched on the side of the wading pool in which she had been placed while her mother hung laundry on the line in their Los Angeles backyard. Upon his daily visits, the scrub jay imparted thoughts to her that she and all humans were other creatures' fools, after which he would fly immediately to the open, back door to seek payment for this knowledge. She remembers her mother compensating the jay regularly with bread crumbs. When Adrienne was older, being a tomboy, she often roamed the aircraft-company-owned, wild canyons a few blocks from her home. Here she received confirmation from blue-bellied and alligator lizards, king snakes, and desert tortoises that the jay had been truthful. As an adult, she had hoped to find that the scrub jay had meant "fool" in a somewhat Shakespearean sense, that is, that humans were wise servants. However, she realizes now that the separation between human and beast lies in the misunderstanding of the concept of "fool." Humans think they are wise, and thus have named their own species so; however, beasts know that, while not wiser than any other species, humans have the capacity to make good servants—but often serve only themselves.